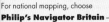

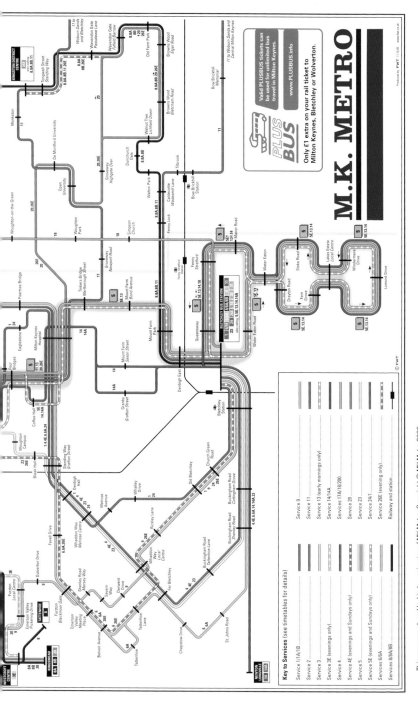

This map reproduced by kind permisssion of MK Metro. Copyright © MK Metro 2006.

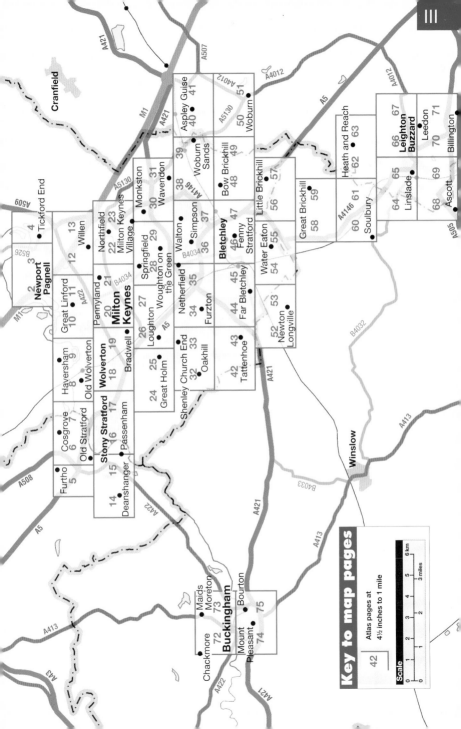

III

Cranfield

Newport Pagnell

Tickford End

Willen

Milton Keynes Village

Northfield

Monkston

Wavendon

Aspley Guise

Woburn Sands

Woburn

Bow Brickhill

Little Brickhill

Heath and Reach

Leighton Buzzard

Leedon

Billington

Linslade

Ascott

Great Brickhill

Soulbury

Springfield

Walton

Simpson

Bletchley

Fenny Stratford

Water Eaton

Milton Keynes

Pennyland

Great Linford

Haversham

Cosgrove

Furtho

Old Stratford

Stony Stratford

Passenham

Wolverton

Old Wolverton

Bradwell

Deanshanger

Great Holm

Shenley Church End

Oakhill

Loughton

Woughton on the Green

Netherfield

Furzton

Far Bletchley

Newton Longville

Tattenhoe

Winslow

Maids Moreton

Bourton

Buckingham

Chackmore

Mount Pleasant

Key to map pages

Atlas pages at
4½ inches to 1 mile

42

Scale

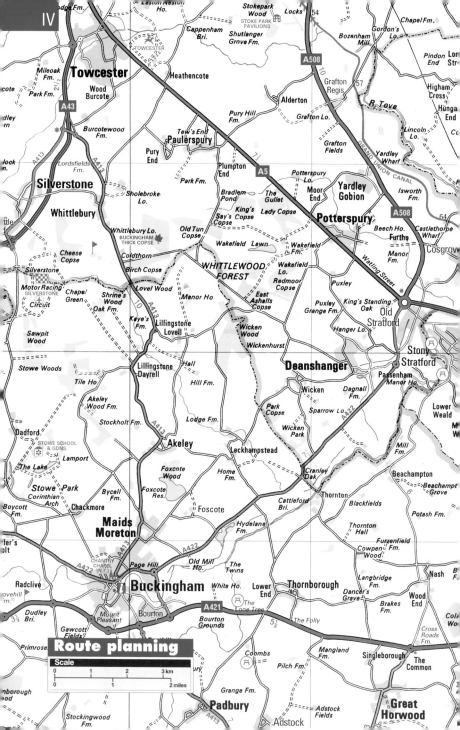

Route planning

Scale

0 — 1 — 2 — 3 km
0 — 1 — 2 miles

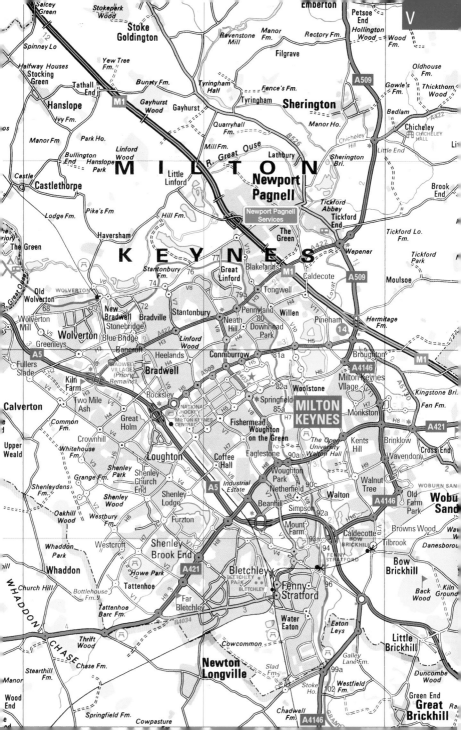

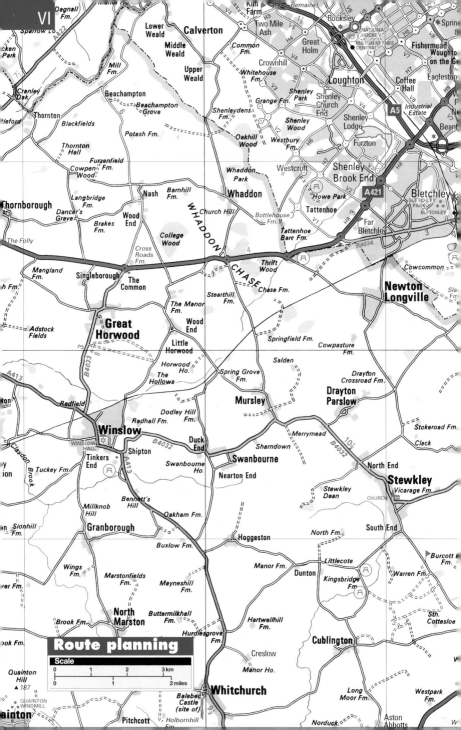

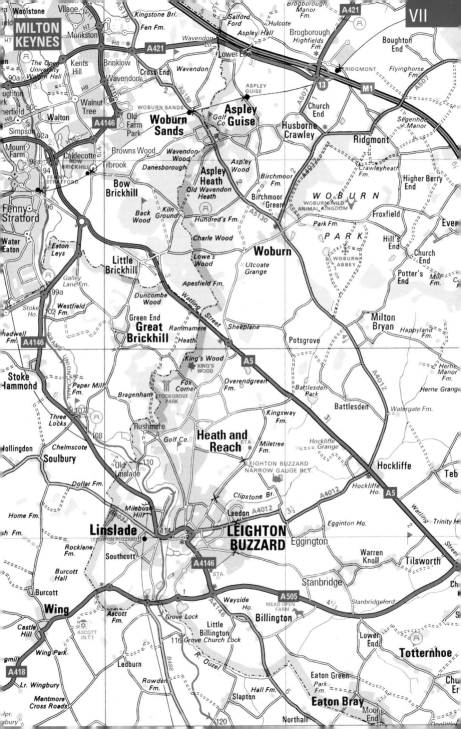

Sights of Milton Keynes

▲ *Xscape, Milton Keynes*

Museums and galleries

Bletchley Park Museum *The Mansion, Bletchley Park, Milton Keynes, MK3 6EB* The site of the famous code-breaking institution, with a Victorian mansion, war-time buildings, exhibitions on war-time communications, code-breaking and code-breaking machines, post-war computers, a collection of 1940s toys, Churchill-related memorabilia. Within the 12 acres of grounds there are also historic vehicles including fire engines, model boats, a model railway exhibition, a children's code trail and a playground (April-October only).
☎01908 640404 🖳www.bletchleypark.org.uk 45 B2

Milton Keynes Gallery *900 Midsummer Boulevard, Central Milton Keynes, MK9 3QA* Contemporary gallery hosting a varied programme of 8–10 exhibitions a year by international artists in all media, including emerging talents.
☎01908 676900
🖳www.mk-g.org 21 A1

Milton Keynes Museum *McConnell Drive, Wolverton, Milton Keynes MK12 5EL* Extensive display of agricultural and industrial machinery, domestic, printing and photographic artefacts tracing the past 200 years of local life. There are also collections of telephones, trams and tractors, and displays with working horses.
☎01908 316222
🖳www.mkmuseum.org.uk 18 B3

Old Gaol Museum *Market Hill, Buckingham, Buckinghamshire, MK18 1JX* Museum housed within one of the oldest standing purpose-built jails in England, constructed in 1748. The collections include fossils, Roman, Saxon, Viking and medieval artefacts, as well as exhibitions on the local lace-making industry, the Royal Buckinghamshire Hussars and Yeomanry, and local author Flora Thompson, who wrote the Lark Rise to Candleford trilogy. There museum also houses temporary exhibitions.
☎01280 823020
🖳www.mkheritage.co.uk/ogb 72 C1

Woburn Heritage Centre Museum *Old St Mary's Church, Bedford Street, Woburn MK17 9PJ* A small museum, in a redundant church, covering the local history of Woburn.
☎01767 682728 51 A1

Historic buildings

All Saints *Church Square, Leighton Buzzard, Bedfordshire, LU7 7TR* The exterior is late 13th century, with the soaring steeple dating back to 1290. The iron strapwork on the door dates is original. The interior (which was skilfully restored after a fire in 1985), is Perpendicular and dates to the 15th century, when new, larger, windows were inserted. The 1980s restoration included as much of the material saved from the fire as possible, for example, several of angels within the complex and beautiful angel

roof. In the chancel, the alabaster reredos shows the crucifixion and the stalls (with misericords) are original. The eagle lectern may be the oldest in England to survive and the font predates the church. Among the large amounts of medieval graffiti is the Simon and Nelly scratch-relief, in which the couple argue over whether a pudding should be boiled or baked. 69 C4

Bancroft Roman Villa *Bancroft Park, off Millers Way, Milton Keynes, MK13* Preserved site of Roman domestic buildings, rediscovered in 1971. On-site interpretation boards explain the layout and what each room was used. for. 19 A3

Bradwell Abbey *off Monks Way (H3), Milton Keynes, MK13 9AP* The site of a 12th-century Benedictine priory, of which a few buildings survive, including the magnificent medieval cruck barn and the 14th-century Chapel of St May. The latter retains some medieval wall paintings. ☎01908 227229 19 A1

Buckingham Chantry Chapel *Market Hill, Buckingham, Buckinghamshire* Romanesque chapel, rebuilt in 1475 and restored in the mid-19th century. One doorway remains from the Romanesque period.
☎01280 823020 72 C1

St Guthlac *Church Street, Passenham, Market Deeping, Northamptonshire* The nave and tower base are 12th century, while the chancel was rebuilt and the interior redecorated and new furnishings installed by Sir Robert Banastre, an Anglo-Catholic courtier to both James I and Charles I. The box pews in the nave and the west gallery are classical in style.The choir stalls in the chancel are arranged as they would have been in a medieval church, with Gothic panelling and misericords, but as elsewhere in the church the classical style predominates. Above the classical choir stall

backs, trompe-l'oeil murals depict prophets and evangelists set within classical niches. These were rediscovered in 1954, having been hidden under whitewash for about 300 years. 16 A1

St Lawrence *Broughton, Milton Keynes, Buckinghamshire* From the outside, St Lawrence's is simply a 14th-century church with an elegant 15th century tower. However, inside, a restoration of 1849 uncovered a beautiful series of wall paintings, including a Pietà and a Doom, as well as St George slaying the Dragon, and St Helena and a set of blacksmith's tools. There are also several interesting memorials and good Victorian stained glass. The building is administered by the Churches Conservation Trust.
🖳www.visitchurches.org.uk 23 B3

St Mary *The Hooke, Willen, Milton Keynes, Buckinghamshire MK15* Built in 1686-70 by Robert Hooke, a colleague of Wren, experimental physicist and inventor of the compound microscope who claimed that Newton had stolen his ideas on gravity, for his old headmaster, Richard Busby. The exterior is classically simple brick with stone dressings. The interior is simple with classical plasterwork including cherubs and acanthus leaves and gilded bosses of suns and shells. The interior furnishings, i.e. the box pews, two-decker pulpit and wooden panelling remain. The cover of the marble font is carved with garlands and fruit. 12 C1

Other sights

Concrete Cows *Off Monks Way (H3), Bancroft, Milton Keynes, Buckinghamshire, MK 13* Milton Keynes' most famous inhabitants were constructed in 1978 by artist residence Liz Leyh with the help of local school children using scrap materials. Over the years they have been

repainted as zebras, given pyjamas, beheaded and kidnapped 19 A2

Entertainment

Theatres, music venues

Milton Keynes Theatre *Marlborough Gate, Central Milton Keynes, Buckinghamshire, MK9 3NZ* A wide range of plays, classical music, opera, comedy, ballet and modern dance and musicals. Box Office 0870 060 6652; 24hr recorded information 01908 547548
www.theambassadors.com 21 A1

Madcap Theatre *Creed Street, Wolverton, Milton Keynes, Buckinghamshire, MK12* Hosts a programme of touring and local theatre, live dance, comedy nights and music, including acoustic music nights. A range of studio- and performance-based workshops in dance, film-making and music, as well as drama groups for all ages. 01908 320173
www.madcap.org.uk 8 C1

The Stables *The Laine Dankworth Centre, Stockwell Lane, Wavendon,* *Milton Keynes, Buckinghamshire, MK17 8LU* Started by Cleo Laine and John Dankworth in 1969, the Stables now boasts a state-of-the-art auditorium with a varied programme of jazz, country, folk, classic rock and pop groups and soloists,big bands, comedy and plays. 01908 280800
www.stables.org 31 A1

Stantonbury Campus Theatre *Purbeck, Stantonbury, Milton Keynes, Buckinghamshire, MK14 6BN* Promotes a high-quality programme of touring, contemporary and children's theatre, musical theatre, big bands, soloists and amateur drama. 01908 324422
www.stantonbury.org.uk 10 B1

Leighton Buzzard Theatre and Cinema *Lake Street, Leighton Buzzard, Bedfordshire, LU7 8RX* Hosts a varied programme of first-run and classic films, as well as pop concerts and musicals by a variety of local theatre groups. 01525 378310
www.leightonbuzzardtheatre.co.uk 66 A1

Cinemas

Cineworld, Xscape *Avebury Boulevard, 602 Marlborough Gate, Central Milton Keynes, Buckinghamshire, MK9 3XZ* 0871 220 8000
www.cineworld.co.uk 21 A1

easyCinema *The Point, Midsummer Boulevard, Central Milton Keynes, Buckinghamshire, MK9 3ND*
www.easyCinema.com 27 B4

Leighton Buzzard Cinema, see Leighton Buzzard Theatre and Cinema 66 A1

Green spaces

Blue Lagoon Local Nature Reserve *near Drayton Road, Bletchley, Milton Keynes, Buckinghamshire, MK3* Disused brickworks with scrub, grassland and lakes. It has a wealth of birds, wild flowers and 30 kinds of butterfly. (Park on Drayton Road). 01908 682590 54 A4

Milton Keynes Parks Trust This organization maintains and cares for nearly 30 parks in and around Milton Keynes, including: **Caldecotte Lake** 37 A/B1 **Elfield Nature Park** 35 A3 **Furzton Lake** 34 C2 **Howe** **Park Wood** 43 B3 **Linford Wood** 20 B3 **Lodge Lake** 26 A3 **North Loughton Valley Park** 19 A2/3 **Shenley Wood** 32 C3 **Willen Lake** 22 B3/4 01908 233600
www.mkparkstrust.co.uk

South Loughton Valley Park 27 A1

Stoney Stratford Nature Reserve 6 C1

Other attractions

Leighton Buzzard Railway *Page's Park Station, Billington Road, Leighton Buzzard, Bedfordshire, LU7 4TN* The Leighton Buzzard Railway is one of the few surviving narrow-gauge light railways in England. It was built in 1919 to serve the local sand-quarrying industry north of the town and the locomotives, wagons and quarrying machinery in the collection reflect this history. There is also an armoured petrol locomotive built for use in the trenches in World War I on loan from the National Railway Museum. Working displays during the operating season. The railway has carried a passenger service, mostly hauled by steam engines, since 1968. The journey – from Page's Park

▼ *The Grand Union Canal near Leighton Buzzard*

to the old Stonehenge Works and back – takes roughly an hour. ℡01525 373888 🖵www.buzzrail.co.uk 70 C3

Activities

Willen Lake and Park *Brickhill Street, Milton Keynes, MK15 0D5* An 80-acre lakeside park and 100-acre lake offering all types of watersports, including water-skiing, wind-surfing, sailing, canoing, wakeboarding and powerboating, as well as cycle hire, fishing, a miniature railway and children's play area and a health club. Seasonal attractions include funfairs and a summer dragonboat spectacular. (See also WakeMK) ℡01908 191620 🖵www.white-cap.co.uk 22 B3/4

Gulliver's Land *Livingstone Drive, Milton Keynes, MK15 0DT* Theme park for families with 40 rides for children between the ages of 2 and 12, including a magic carpet, ferris wheel and log flume. Also a train, crazy golf,

▼ *The Point, Milton Keynes*

face-painting and regular shows. ℡01908 609001 🖵www.gulliversfun.co.uk 22 A2

Xscape *602 Marlborough Gate, Central Milton Keynes, Buckinghamshire, MK9 3XS* As well as a multiplex (see Cineworld) and health studios (see Virgin Active), this modern complex houses:
Real Snow Slopes – skiing ℡0871 2225670
Airkix – vertical windtunnel in which visitors can experience the sensation of flight ℡0845 3316549
Mid City Lanes – 10-pin 'glow' bowling ℡01908 295222
Climb Zone – with two indoor walls ℡01908 237748 ℡0871 200 3220 🖵www.xscape. co.uk 21 A1
Planet Ice, Leisure Plaza *Elder Gate, Central Milton Keynes, MK9 1BL* Ice rink offering figure skating, ice karting and after schools sessions, as well as evening events for adults. ℡01908 696696 🖵www.planet-ice.co.uk 27 A2

Watersports

Haversham Sailing Club *24 High Street, Haversham, Milton Keynes* Family oriented private sailing club, with racing, sail training and an under 16s section. ℡01908 225657 🖵http://homepages.rya-online.net/hsc123 9 C4

Milton Keynes Rowing Club *Monellan Grove, Caldecotte, Milton Keynes, Buckinghamshire, MK7* Friendly and growing rowing club with mens' womens' and juniors' sections, for both beginners and racers alike. 🖵www.mkrowing.org 47 B4

Milton Keynes Sailing Club *Monellan Grove, Caldecotte, Milton Keynes, Buckinghamshire, MK7* Family oriented sailing club, with racing, race training, safety courses and youth section. 🖵www.milton-keynes-sc.fsnet.co.uk 47 B4

WakeMK Wakeboard and Waterski Centre *The Cable Building, Willen Lake, Brickhill Street (V10), Milton Keynes, Buckinghamshire, MK15 9HQ*

Centre offering facilities for surfing and kitesurving, kneeboarding, wakeboarding and waterskiing for all levels of ability. ℡01908 670197 🖵www.wakeMK.com 22 B3

Footpaths and trails

Grand Union Canal Walk Following the towpath of this canal, and its branches, from Paddington in London to Birmingham, this long-distance walk skirts the eastern edge of Milton Keynes. North and south of the city, the landscape is more rural.

Greensand Ridge Walk *Starting in Linslade,* this 64-km (40-mile) walk follows a ridge of Lower Greensand stone that has been quarried locally for building for centuries. It is characterised by gently rolling hills and small valleys. In parts it is heavily wooded with conifers but there are remnants of ancient woodland, acid grassland and heathland. There are also wet meadows where the hills are cut by the Ouzel and Flit rivers. 🖵www.greensand-trust. org.uk

Golf courses

Abbey Hill Golf Centre *Monks Way, Two Mile Ash, Milton Keynes, Buckinghamshire, MK8 8AA* An 18-hole SSS course with an SSS of 69, together with a 6-hold par-3 course practice area. Visitors welcome. ℡01908 563845 🖵www.abbeyhillgc.co.uk 18 B1

Aspley Guise and Woburn Sands Golf Club *West Hill, Aspley Guise, Buckinghamshire, MK17 8DX* 18-hole course with an SSS of 71 set in undulating parkland. Visitors should contact the club in advance for restrictions. ℡01234 826100 40 B2

Leighton Buzzard Golf Club *Plantation Road, Leighton Buzzard, Bedfordshire, LU7 7JF* An 18-hole course with an SSS of 70 set in wooded parkland. Practice ground. Visitors should contact the club in advance for restrictions. ℡01525 244800 🖵www.leightonbuzzardgolf. net 62 B1

Three Locks Golf Club *Great Brickhill, Milton Keynes, Buckinghamshire, MK17 9BH* 18-hole parkland course with an SSS of 71, renowned for the water hazards created by the River Ouzel, which runs through the area. Practice ground. Visitors welcome. ☎01525 270050 🖳www.threelocksgolfclub.co.uk 60 C4

Windmill Hill Golf Centre *Tattenhoe Lane, Bletchley, Milton Keynes, Buckinghamshire, MK3 7RB* Flat parkland championship 18-hole SSS 72 course designed by Henry Cotton. Floodlit driving range. Visitors should book 7 days in advance. Also home of Windmill Hill Tennis and Golf Academy. ☎01908 631113 🖳www.windmillhill.co.uk 44 A2

Woburn Golf and Country Club *Little Brickhill, Milton Keynes, Buckinghamshire, MK17 9LJ* Three courses set among rolling parkland on the Buckinghamshire/Bedfordshire border: the Duke's course is has an SSS of 74, while the Duchess' and Marquess courses have SSSs of 72. Visitors welcome weekdays by prior arrangement. ☎01908 370756 🖳www.woburngolf.co.uk 49 A1

Leisure centres and fitness clubs

Bletchley Leisure Centre *Princes Way, Bletchley, Buckinghamshire, MK2 2HQ* Facilities include swimming pools, indoor bowls centre, gymnasium, squash courts, floodlit outdoor football, netball and tennis areas, and a fitness club. ☎01908 377251 46 B2

Brook End Sports Centre *Walbank Grove, Shenley Brook End, Milton Keynes, MK5 7ZT* Sports centre open to the public outside school hours, offering indoor volleyball, badminton, basketball, 5-a-side football and short tennis and outdoor hardcourts for basketball, tennis and short tennis, volleyball and netball, football pitches, outdoor artificial cricket wicket, indoor cricket nets and a dance studio. ☎01908 330110 33 B1

Holmes Place Health Club *National Badminton Centre, Bradwell Road, Loughton Lodge, Milton Keynes, Buckinghamshire, MK8 9LA* Private health club offering fitness studios, aerobics and step aerobics, pilates, sauna, cycling and spinning, and yoga. ☎01908 578 300 🖳www.holmesplace.com 26 A3

David Lloyd Club *Livingstone Drive, Newlands, Milton Keynes, Buckinghamshire, MK15 0DL* Private health and racquets club offering tennis, badminton and squash courts, swimming pools, gymnasium and spa. ☎01908 207900 🖳www.davidlloydleisure.co.uk 22 A3

Middleton Swimming Pool *Tickford Street, Newport Pagnell, Buckinghamshire, MK16 9BG* A modern 33-metre pool offering a variety of public swimming sessions as well as normal public swimming out of school hours. ☎01908 610477 🖳http://newport-pagnell.org.uk/Swimming_Intro.htm 4 A1

Shenley Leisure Centre *Burchard Crescent, Shenley Church End, Milton Keynes, Buckinghamshire, MK5 6HF* Community-based leisure centre with facilities including a sports hall, gymnasium, fitness room, dance studio, squash courts and floodlit artificial pitches. ☎01908 502488 🖳www.shenleyleisure.org.uk 26 A1

Stantonbury Leisure Centre *Stantonbury Campus, Saxon Street, Milton Keynes, MK14 6BN* Facilities include 2 sports halls, tennis and netball courts, a dance studio, 2 swimming pools, floodlit artificial pitches and athletics track, 11 badminton courts and a health club. ☎01908 324466 🖳www.stantonbury.org.uk 10 B1

Swan Pool & Leisure Centre *London Road, Buckingham, Buckinhamshire, MK18 1AE* Facilities offered include a six-lane main pool and a learner pool, a dance studio, 2 squash courts, an all-weather pitch and a gymnasium ☎01280 817500 74 C3

Tiddenfoot Leisure Centre *Mentmore Road, Leighton Buzzard, Bedfordshire, LU7 7PA* A community leisure centre, offering swimming lessons for all ages, and other sports such as kick-boxing and karate. ☎01525 375765 69 B3

Virgin Active *Xscape, 602 Marlborough Gate, Central Milton Keynes, Buckinghamshire, MK9 3XS* Fully equipped fitness rooms, personal training, dedicated spin studio, 2-class studio, pool and spa area. ☎01908 298800 🖳www.virginactive.co.uk 21 A1

Watling Way Centre *Galley Hill, Stony Stratford, Milton Keynes, Buckinghamshire, MK11 1PA* Indoor pool and hall offering swimming courses. ☎01908 562257 17 A3

Wolverton Pool *Aylesbury Street, West Wolverton, Milton Keynes, Buckinghamshire, MK12 5BS* An outdoor three-pool complex open from the end of May to the beginning of September depending on the weather. ☎01908 312091 18 A4

Woughton Leisure Centre *Rainbow Drive, Chaffron Way, Leadenhall, Milton Keynes, Buckinghamshire, MK6 5EJ* The centre offers two sports halls, a gymnasium, health club, playing fields, dance studio and floodlit tennis courts. Some facilities are only available outside school hours. ☎01908 660392 🖳www.woughtoncentre.co.uk 27 C1

Other sports

National Badminton Centre *Bradwell Road, Loughton Lodge, Milton Keynes, Buckinghamshire, MK8 9LA* Members club for those with at least basic badminton skills. Courts are available for hire by local players. ☎01908 578300 🖳www.theNBC.co.uk 26 A3

Bletchley RUFC *Manor Field Sports Ground, Bletchley, Milton Keynes, Buckinghamshire, MK2 2HX* Local rugby club with 3 full-sized pitches and seniors, colts, juniors, midi and mini teams. ☎01908 372298 🖳www.bletchleyrugby.com 47 A2

Buckingham Rugby Club *Floyd Field (off Duck Lake), Maids Moreton, Buckingham, Buckinghamshire, MK18 1RF* Local club with seniors, ladies and youth teams.

☎01280 815474 🖳www.buckinghamrugby.co.uk 73 A3

Milton Keynes Rugby Club *Field Lane, Greenleys, Milton Keynes, MK12 6AZ* Local rugby club with seniors, juniors, colts, women, midis and minis teams. ☎01908 313858 🖳www.mkrufc.com 17 C3

Berks and Bucks Football Association For details of football teams playing in a variety of local leagues. ☎01367 242099 🖳www.berks-bucksfa.com

Other information

Silverlink County ☎0845 6014868 🖳www.silverlink-trains.com

Virgin West Coast ☎0870 7891234 🖳www.virgintrains.co.uk

Traveline Public Transport Information ☎08706 6082608 (+ code 820) 🖳www.travelline.co.uk

National Rail Enquiries ☎08457 48 49 50 🖳http://nrekb.nationalrail.co.uk/

Arriva The Shires and Essex ☎01923 682262 🖳www.arrivabus.co.uk

MK Metro ☎01908 225100 🖳www.askmk.com/mkmetro.mkmetro.html

Buckingham Town Bus Services ☎0870 6082608 🖳www.buckscc.gov.uk/travelinfo

United Counties ☎01604 601502 🖳www.stagecoach-bus.com

Car parks and parking ☎01908 252224 🖳www.mkweb.co.uk/parking

Buckingham TIC *, within the Old Gaol Museum, Market Hill, Buckingham, Buckinghamshire, MK18 1JX* ☎01280 823020 72 C1

Milton Keynes TIC *, 890 Midsummer Boulevard, Central Milton Keynes, Buckinghamshire* ☎01908 558300 21 A1

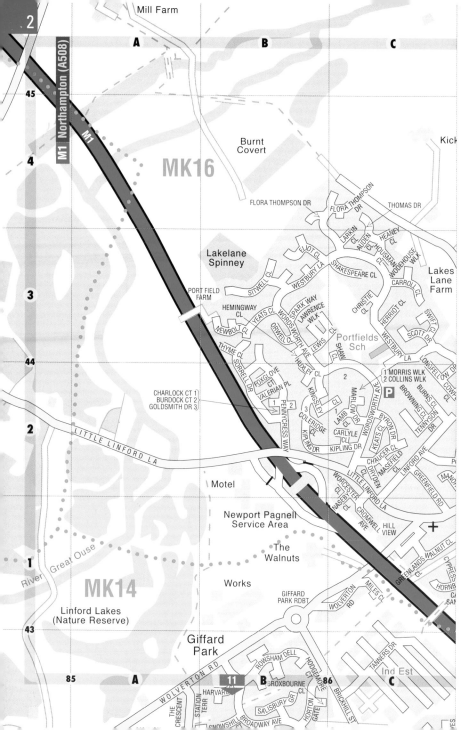

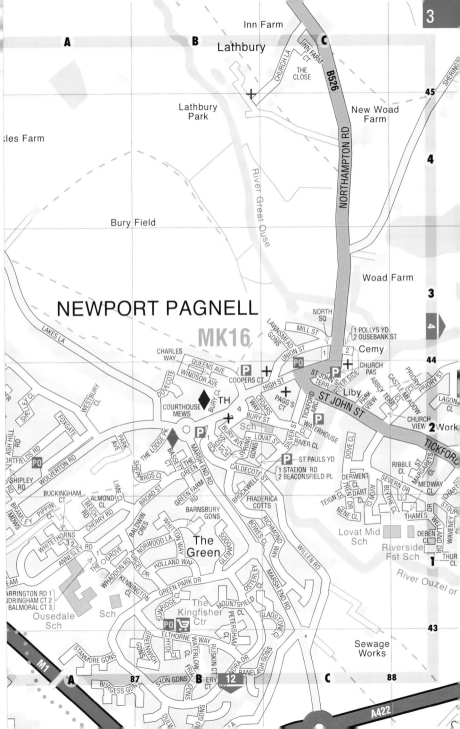

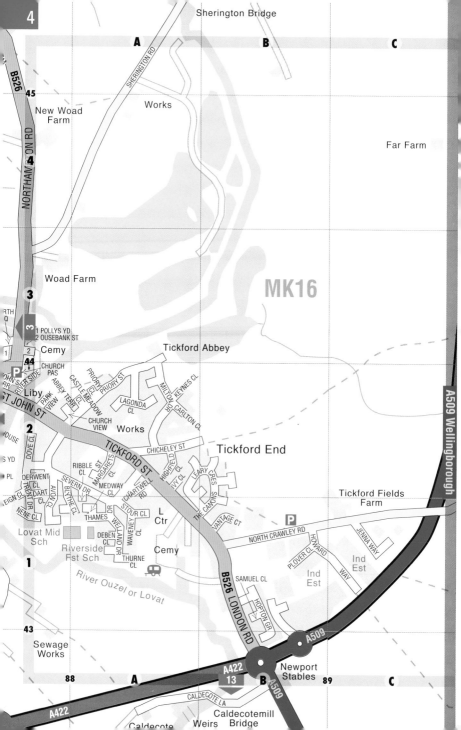

4

Sherington Bridge

A   B   C

B526

SHERINGTON RD

45

New Woad Farm

Works

NORTHAMPTON RD

4

Far Farm

Woad Farm

3

MK16

NORTH
Q

3

1 POLLYS YD
2 OUSEBANK ST

Cemy

Tickford Abbey

44

CHURCH PAS

P

RIVERSIDE

JOHN'S
RR

Liby

ST JOHN ST

PARK VIEW

ABBEY TERR

CASTLE MEADOW

PRIORY DR

PRIORY ST

MILTON RD

KEYNES CL

CARLTON CL

2

HOUSE

DOVE CL

CHURCH VIEW

LAGONDA CL

Works

Tickford End

S YD

TICKFORD ST

CHICHELEY ST

PL

DERWENT CL

RIBBLE CL

ST MARGARET'S

HIGHFIELD CL

IVY CL

LEARY CRES

Tickford Fields Farm

REIGN CL

TRENT DR

DART CL

SEVERN DR

BLYTHE CL

MEDWAY CL

CHARTWELL RD

THE CANOVAS

VANTAGE CT

AVON CL

NENE CL

THAMES CL

STOUR CL

L Ctr

NORTH CRAWLEY RD

P

JENNA WAY

Lovat Mid Sch

WELLAND DR

WAVENEY DR

DEBEN CL

Cemy

PLOVER CL

HOWARD WAY

Ind Est

Riverside Fst Sch

THURNE CL

Ind Est

1

SAMUEL CL

River Ouzel or Lovat

B526 LONDON RD

HOPTON GR

43

Sewage Works

A422
13

A509

A509

Newport Stables

88   A   B   89   C

A422

CALDECOTE LA

A509

Caldecote

Caldecotemill Bridge

Weirs

A509 Wellingborough

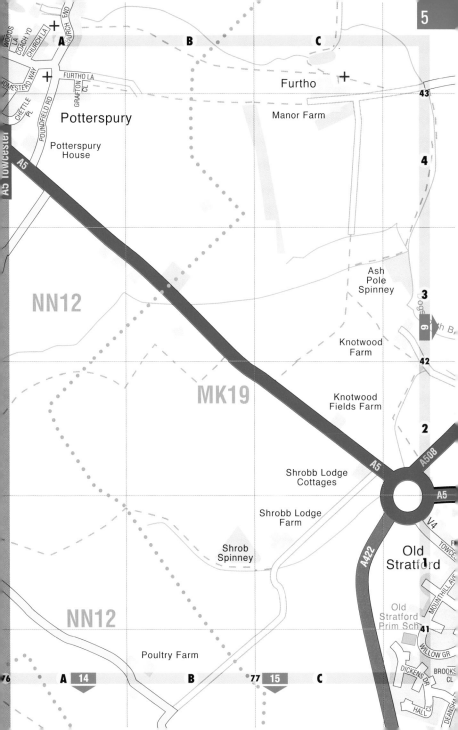

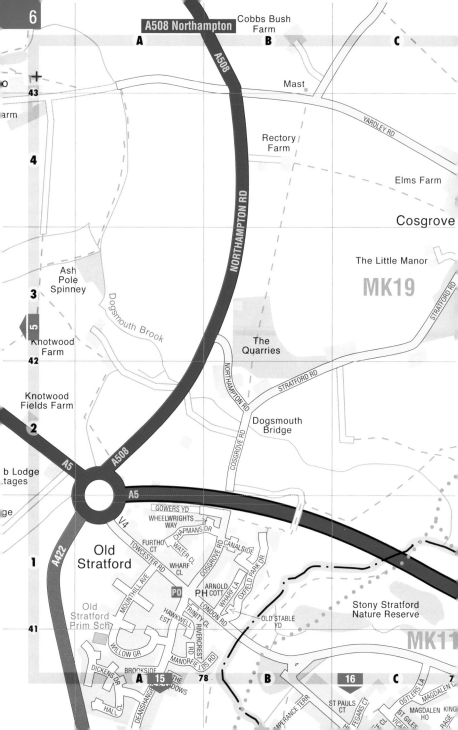

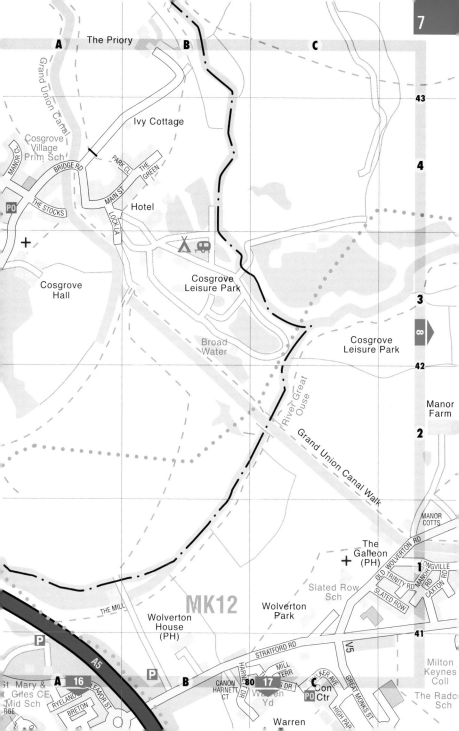

The Priory

A

B

C

43

4

Grand Union Canal

Ivy Cottage

Cosgrove
Village
Prim Sch

MANOR CL

BRIDGE RD

PARK CL

THE GREEN

MAIN ST

LOCK LA

PO

THE STOCKS

Hotel

Cosgrove
Hall

Cosgrove
Leisure Park

Broad
Water

3

8

Cosgrove
Leisure Park

42

River Great Ouse

Manor
Farm

2

Grand Union Canal Walk

MANOR
COTTS

The
Galleon
(PH)

OLD WOLVERTON RD

OLD TRINITY RD

WOLVERTON RD

MANOR RD

LONGVILLE

CAXTON RD

1

Slated Row
Sch

SLATED ROW

Wolverton
Park

THE MILL

MK12

Wolverton
House
(PH)

STRATFORD RD

V5

41

P

A5

P

St Mary &
Giles CE
Mid Sch

RGE

A

16

RYELAND

LEAMOR ST

BRETON

P

B

CANON
HARNETT
CT

HARNETT DR

MILL
TERR

80

17

S DR

Warren
Yd

WALKER AVE

PO

C

Con
Ctr

GREAT MONKS ST

HIGH PAR

Milton
Keynes
Coll

The Radc
Sch

Warren

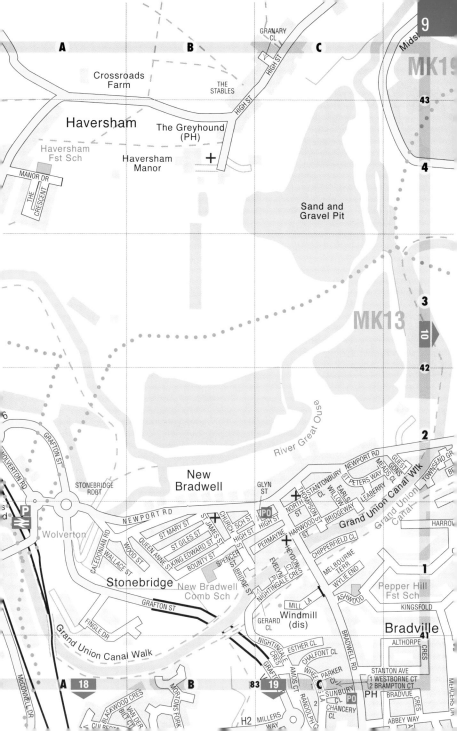

Granary CL

High ST

Midsl

MK19

A

B

C

43

Crossroads Farm

THE STABLES

Haversham

The Greyhound (PH)

4

HIGH ST

Haversham Fst Sch

Haversham Manor

MANOR DR

THE CRESCENT

Sand and Gravel Pit

MK13

3

10

42

River Great Ouse

2

New Bradwell

WOLVERTON RD

GRAFTON ST

STONEBRIDGE RDBT

Newport Rd

Newport Rd

NEWPORT RD

GLYN ST

STANTONBURY CL

THOMPSON ST

NORTH ST

EARLS CL

ST PETERS WAY

WILLOW

LEABERRY

MEADS CL

GUEST GDNS

TOWNSEND GR

Grand Union Canal Wlk

Grand Union Canal

HARROW

P

Wolverton

CALEDONIAN RD

WOOD ST

QUEEN ANNE ST

WALLACE ST

KING EDWARD ST

ST MARY ST

ST GILES ST

ST JAMES ST

BOUNTY ST

SPENCER ST

CHURCH ST

SCH ST

HIGH ST

ST BRIDGE ST

PERMAYNE

HARWOOD ST

BRIDGEWAY

HEYDONS CL

CHIPPERFIELD CL

MELBOURNE TERR

WYLIE END

PO

Stonebridge

New Bradwell Comb Sch

GRAFTON ST

FINGLE DR

EVELYN CL

NIGHTINGALE CRES

MILL LA

ASHWOOD

Windmill (dis)

GERARD CL

Pepper Hill Fst Sch

KINGSFOLD

Bradville

1

41

ALTHORPE CRES

Grand Union Canal Walk

MCCONNELL DR

NIGHTINGALE CRES

GRAFTON ST

ESTHER CL

CHALFONT CL

WHE

PARKER CL

BRADWELL RD

STANTON AVE

1 WESTBORNE CT
2 BRAMPTON CT

MERCERS DR

A

18

B

83

19

C

MORTONS FORK

BLACKWOOD CRES

VAN DER BILT CT

GILBERT

AMOS CL

RANDOLPH CL

H2

MILLERS WAY

SUNBURY CL

PO

CHANCERY CL

PH

BRADVUE CRES

ABBEY WAY

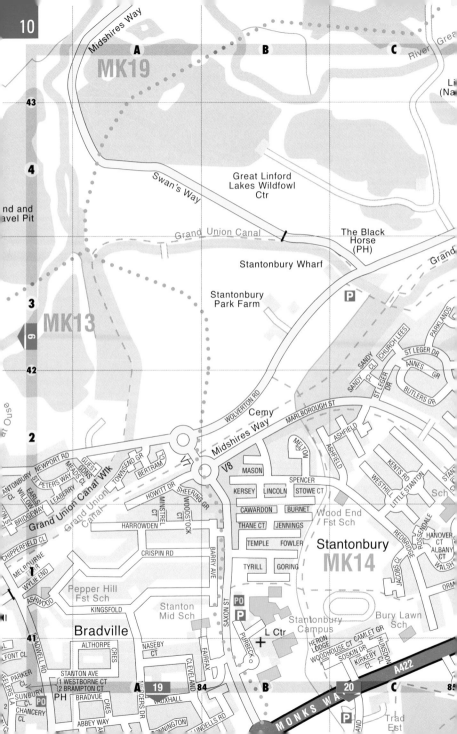

MK19

A   B   C

River Gree

43

4

Swan's Way

Great Linford
Lakes Wildfowl
Ctr

nd and
avel Pit

Grand Union Canal

The Black
Horse
(PH)

Grand

Stantonbury Wharf

3

MK13

Stantonbury
Park Farm

P

PARKLANDS

42

CHURCH LEES

ST LEGER DR

SANDY CL

ST LEGER
DR

ANNES
GR

BUTLERS GR

SANDY

at Ouse

WOLVERTON RD

Cemy

Midshires Way

MARLBOROUGH ST

ASHFIELD

2

V7

V8

MELTON

ASHFIELD

WESTHILL

KENTS RD

LITTLE STANTON

Sch

NEWPORT RD

ANTONBURY
CL

ST PETERS WAY

GUEST
GDNS

MEADS CT

TOWNSEND GR

BERTRAM

MASON

SPENCER

KERSEY   LINCOLN   STOWE CT

Wood End
Fst Sch

REDBRIDGE

ROSENDALE

HANOVER
CT

ALBANY
CT

WALSH

Grand Union Canal Wlk

EARLS
WILLOW

LEABERRY

BRIDGEWAY

HOWITT DR

MINSTREL
CT

SHEERING GR

WOODSTOCK

CAWARDON

BURNET

THANE CT   JENNINGS

Stantonbury

MK14

JACOBS CL

CHIPPERFIELD CL

HARROWDEN

TEMPLE   FOWLER

ORM

CRISPIN RD

BARRY AVE

TYRILL   GORING

MELBOURNE
PER

1

Pepper Hill
Fst Sch

KINGSFOLD

Stanton
Mid Sch

SAXON ST

PO

L Ctr

Stantonbury
Campus

Bury Lawn
Sch

WYLIE END

ASHWOOD

P

HERON
LODGE

CAMLET GR

HUNSDON
CL

41

FONT CL

ADWELL RD

PARKER
CL

ALTHORPE

NASEBY
CT

FAIRFAX

CLEVELAND

PURBECK

WOODHOUSE CT

SOSKIN DR

KIRKEBY
CL

A422

STANTON AVE

Bradville

19   84

P

85

SUNBURY
CL

PO

PH

1 WESTBORNE CT
2 BRAMPTON CT

BRADVUE

CRES

A   19   84   B   20   C

CHANCERY
CL

ABBEY WAY

VAUXHALL

LINDELLS RD

MONKS WA

P

Trad
Est

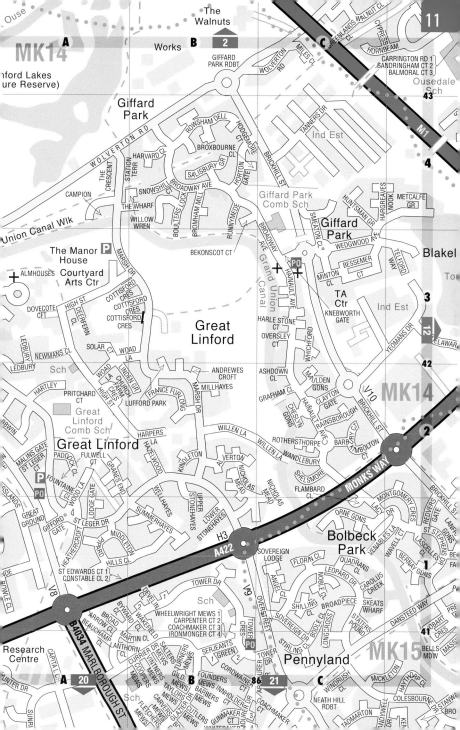

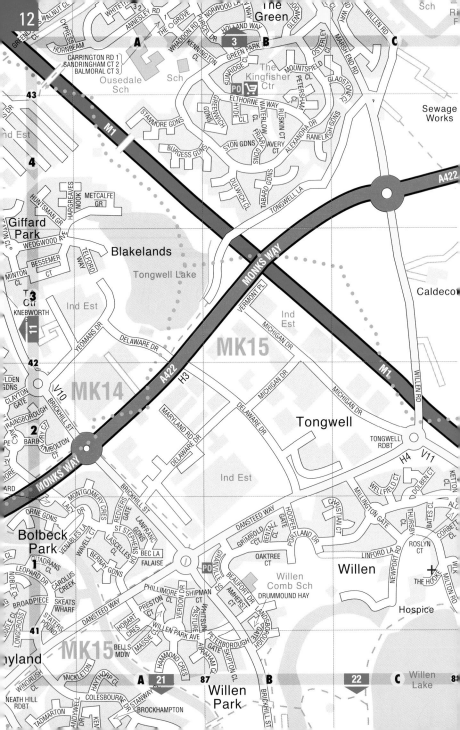

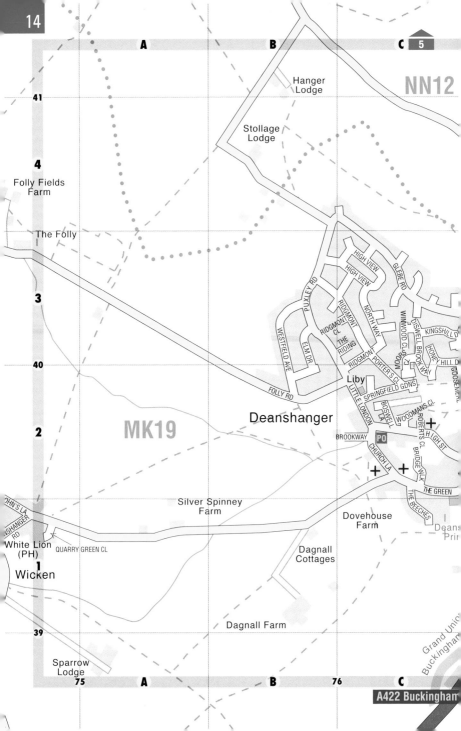

NN12

Hanger
Lodge

41

Stollage
Lodge

4

Folly Fields
Farm

The Folly

HIGH VIEW

HIGH VIEW

GLEBE RD

3

PUXLEY RD

RIDGMONT CL

NORTH WAY

WINWOOD CL

BISWELL BROOK WAY

KINGSHILL D

GOOSE MDW

ELM DR

RIDGMONT

THE
RIDING

MOORS

HONEY HILL D

WESTFIELD AVE

PORTER'S CL

40

RIDGMONT

FOLLY RD

Liby

SPRINGFIELD GDNS

LITTLE LONDON

WOODMANS CL

MK19

Deanshanger

BISWELL

ROBERTS CL

2

BROOKWAY

PO

HIGH ST

CHURCH LA

BRIDGE WLK

THE GREEN

Silver Spinney
Farm

Dovehouse
Farm

THE BEECHES

Deans
Prin

JOHN'S LA

SHANGER
RD

White Lion
(PH)

QUARRY GREEN CL

Dagnall
Cottages

1

Wicken

39

Dagnall Farm

Grand Unio
Buckingham

Sparrow
Lodge

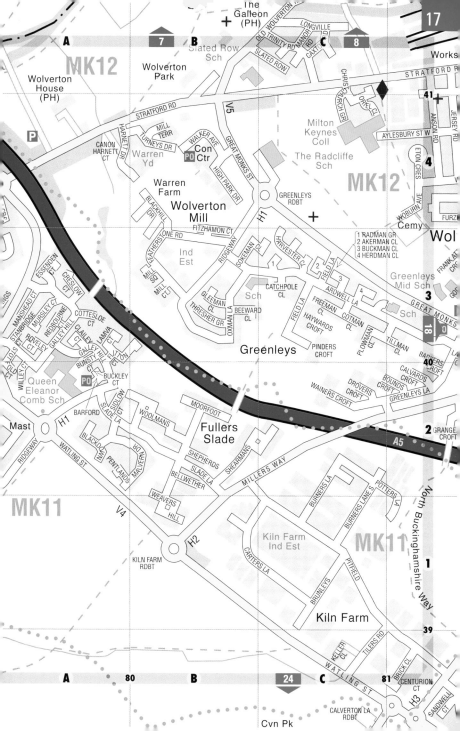

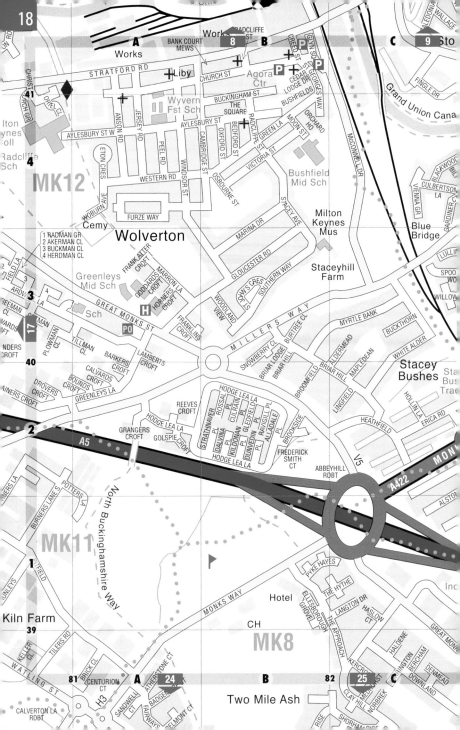

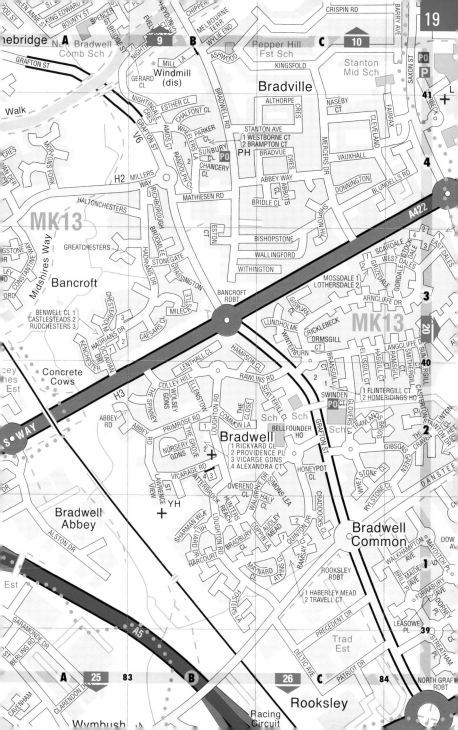

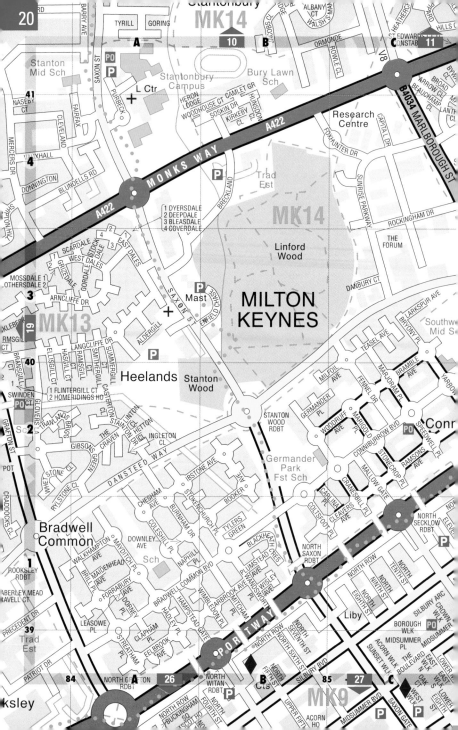

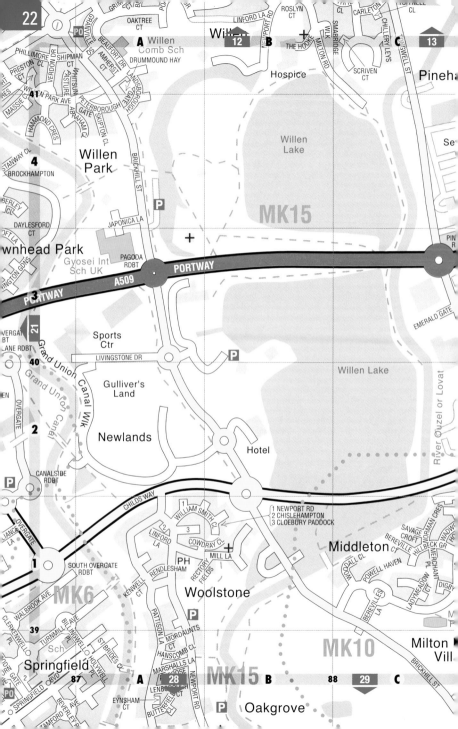

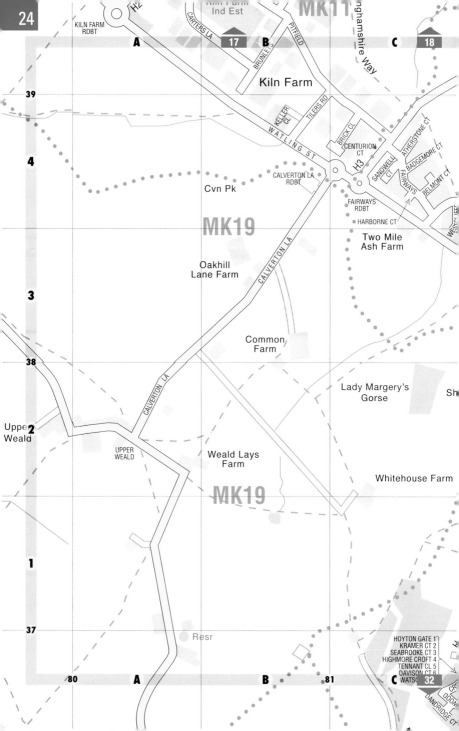

H2

Kiln Farm
Ind Est

MK11

nghamshire Way

BRUNLEYS

Kiln Farm

39

TILERS RD

KELLER CL

WATLING ST

BRICK CL

CENTURION
CT

ATHERSTONE CT

BADGEMORE CT

4

H3

SANDWELL CT

FAIRWAYS

BELMONT CT

Cvn Pk

CALVERTON LA
RDBT

FAIRWAYS
RDBT

WEST TER

MK19

HARBORNE CT

Two Mile
Ash Farm

Oakhill
Lane Farm

CALVERTON LA

3

Common
Farm

38

Lady Margery's
Gorse

Sh

CALVERTON LA

Uppe **2**
Weald

UPPER
WEALD

Weald Lays
Farm

Whitehouse Farm

MK19

1

37

Resr

HOYTON GATE 1
KRAMER CT 2
SEABROOKE CT 3
HIGHMORE CROFT 4
TENNANT CL 5
DAVISON CT 6
WATS

DANDRIDGE CT

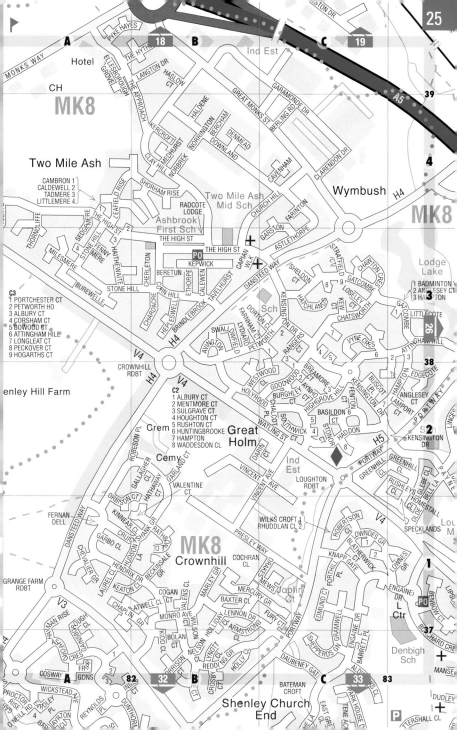

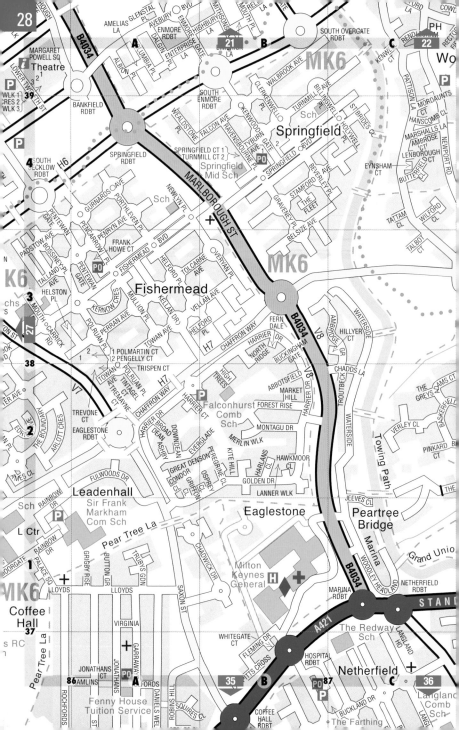

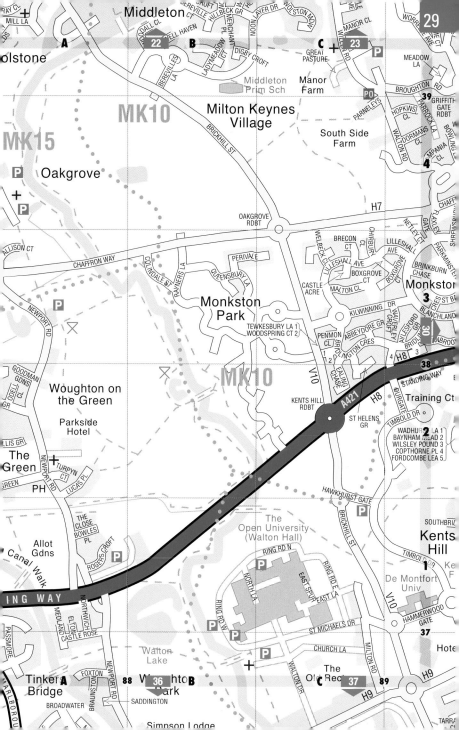

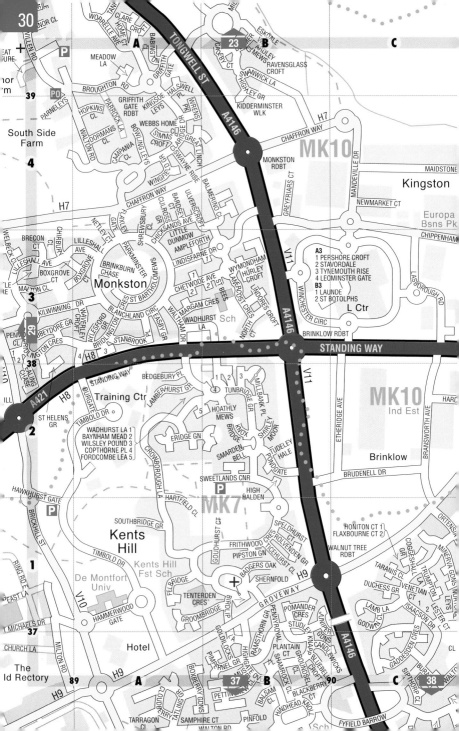

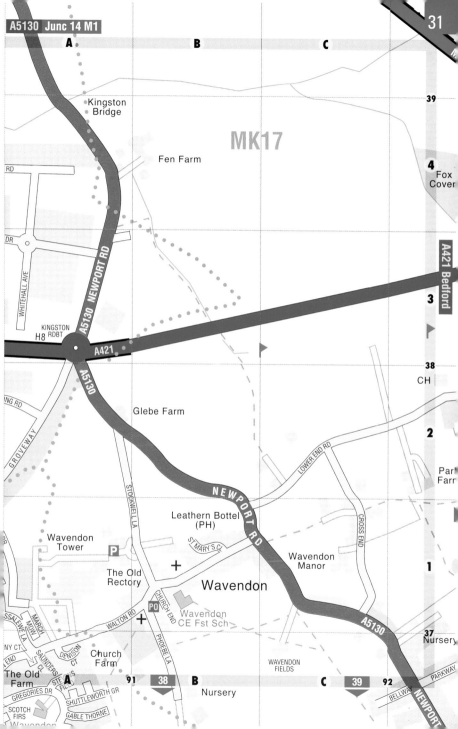

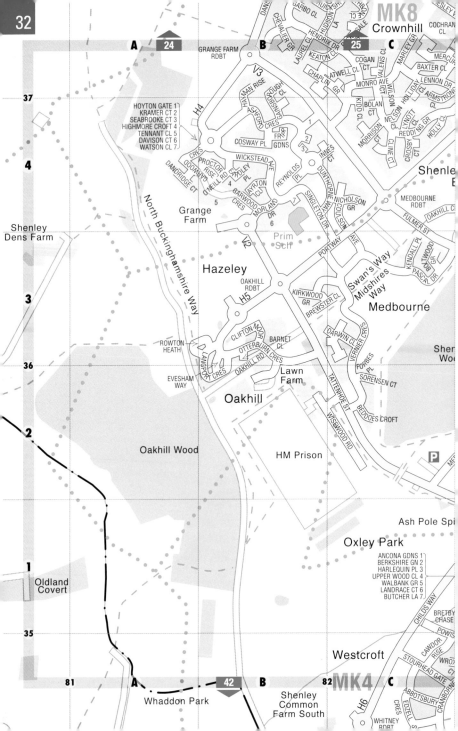

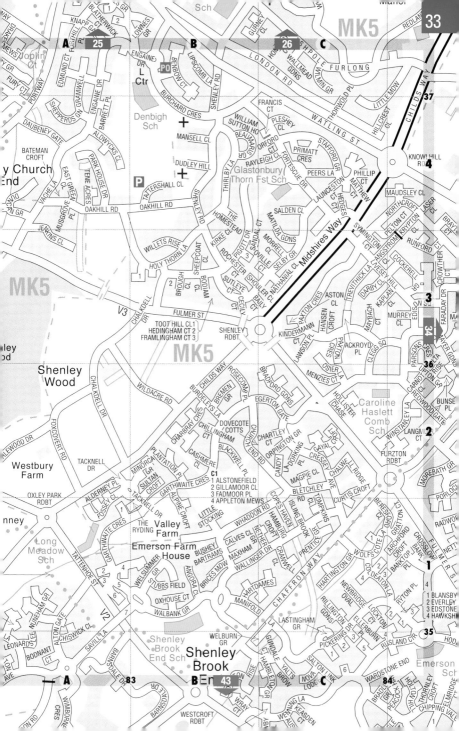

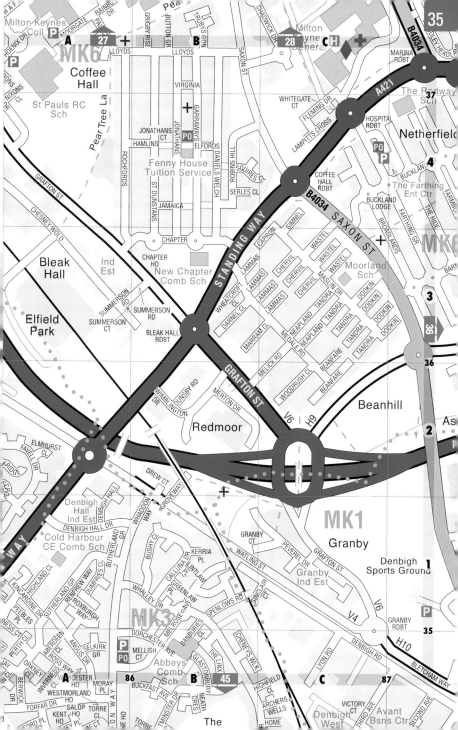

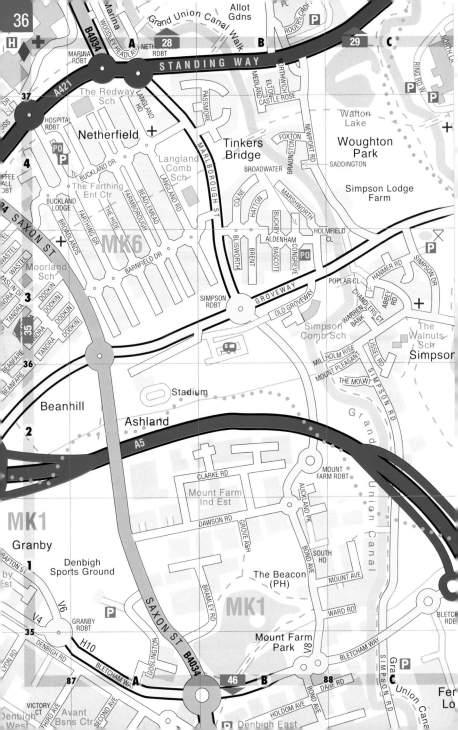

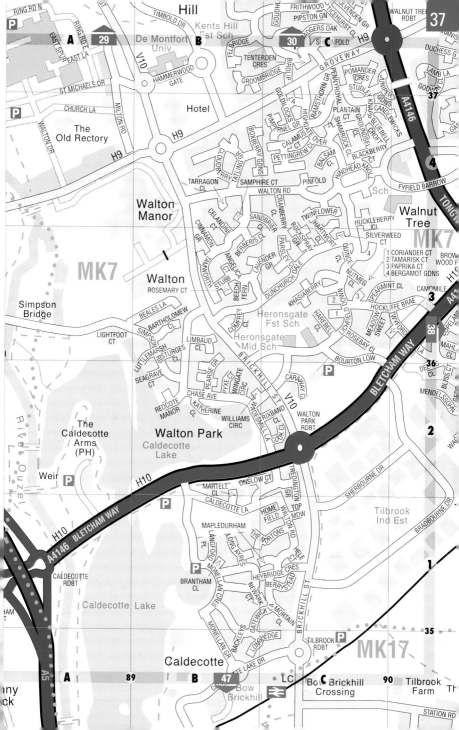

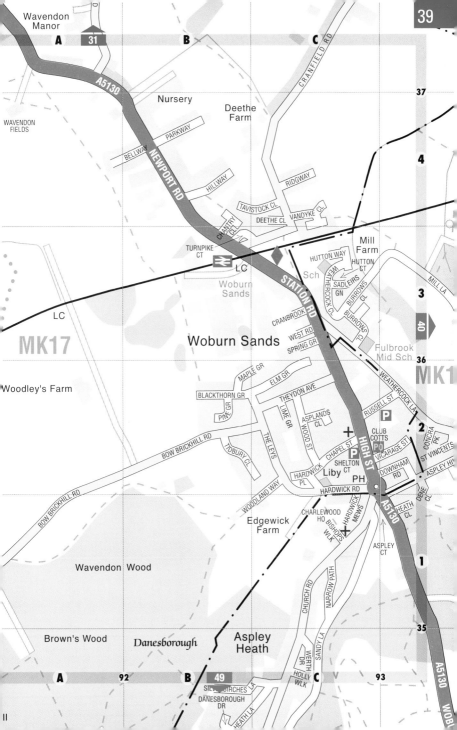

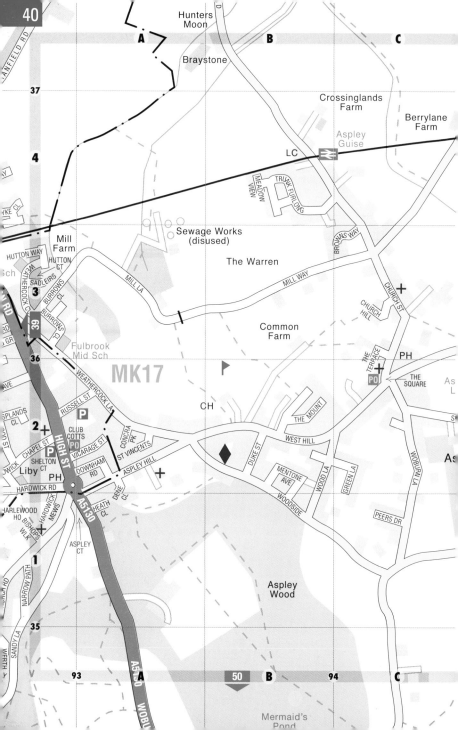

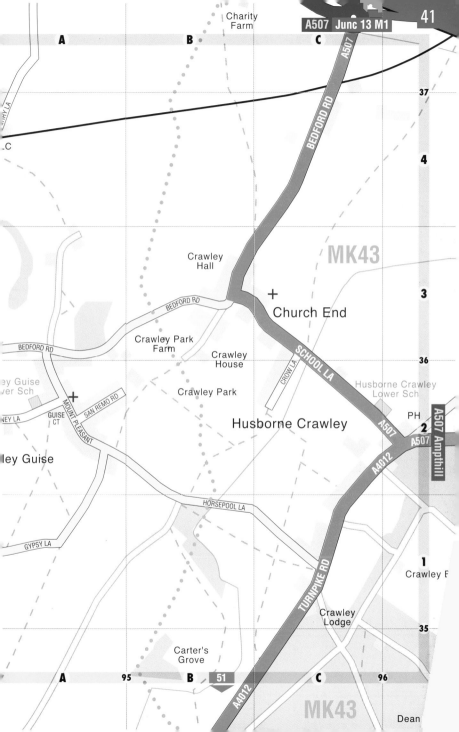

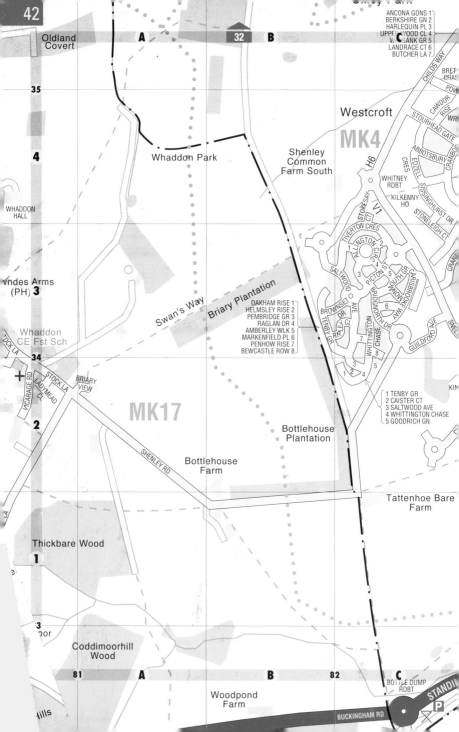

Oldland
Covert

A

32

B

ANCONA GDNS 1
BERKSHIRE GN 2
HARLEQUIN PL 3
UPPERWOOD CL 4
V. BANK GR 5
LANDRACE CT 6
BUTCHER LA 7

C

35

4

WHADDON
HALL

vndes Arms
(PH) **3**

Whaddon
CE Fst Sch

34

2

Whaddon Park

Shenley
Common
Farm South

Westcroft

MK4

WHITNEY
RDBT

KILKENNY
HO

CHILDS WAY

BRET
CHAS

POW

CANDOR
RISE

WR

STOURHEAD GATE

H6

ABBOTSBURY

CRES

EDZELL

CRANB

STONELEIGH CT

SISSINGHURST DR

STOKESAY

V1

TIVERTON CRES

ALLINGTON CIRC

SALTWOOD

PICTON

SOUTH GR

CARISBROOKE WAY

CRAN

GUILDFORD AVE

SNE

Swan's Way

Briary Plantation

OAKHAM RISE 1
HELMSLEY RISE 2
PEMBRIDGE GR 3
RAGLAN DR 4
AMBERLEY WLK 5
MARKENFIELD PL 6
PENHOW RISE 7
BEWCASTLE ROW 8

BROWNSET
GR

TENBY GR

RA
CL

NEWINGTON
DR

WHITTINGTON
CHASE

BRIDGNORTH DR

KIM

1 TENBY GR
2 CAISTER CT
3 SALTWOOD AVE
4 WHITTINGTON CHASE
5 GOODRICH GN

MK17

STOCK LA

VICARAGE RD

LADYMEAD CL

STOCK LA

BRIARY
VIEW

SHENLEY RD

Bottlehouse
Farm

Bottlehouse
Plantation

Tattenhoe Bare
Farm

Thickbare Wood

1

3
oor

Coddimoorhill
Wood

81

A

B

82

C

Woodpond
Farm

BUCKINGHAM RD

BOTTLE DUMP
RDBT

STANDI

Hills

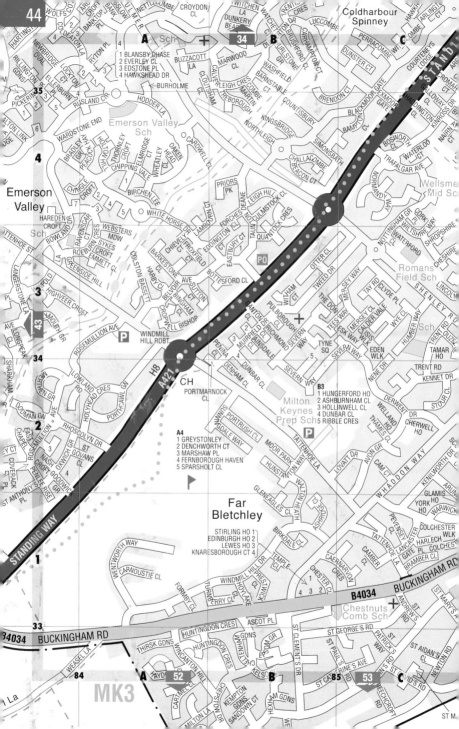

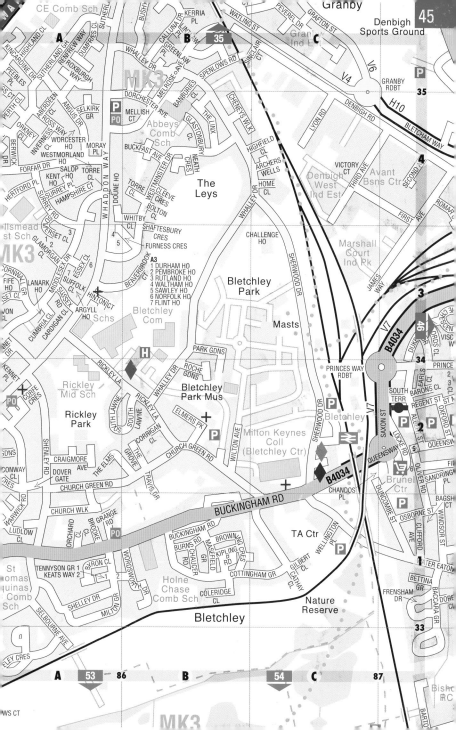

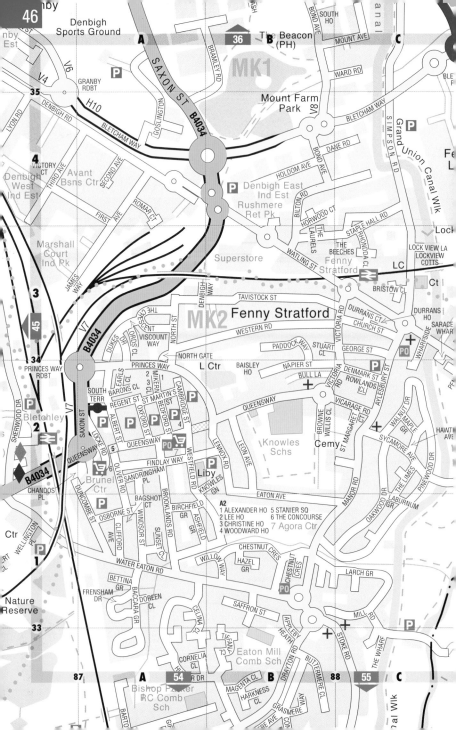

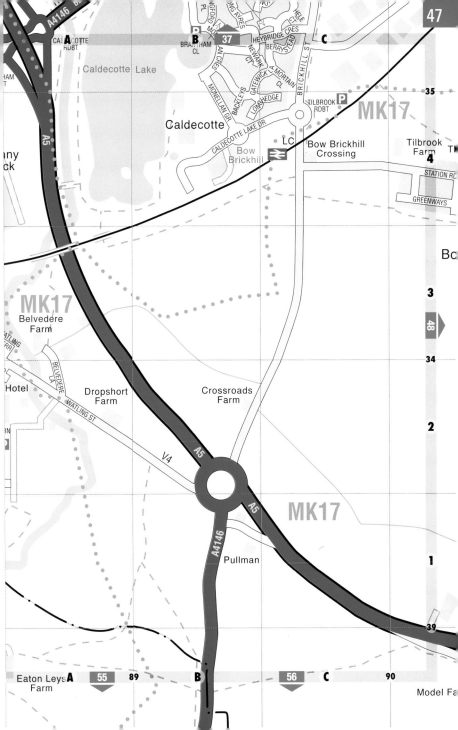

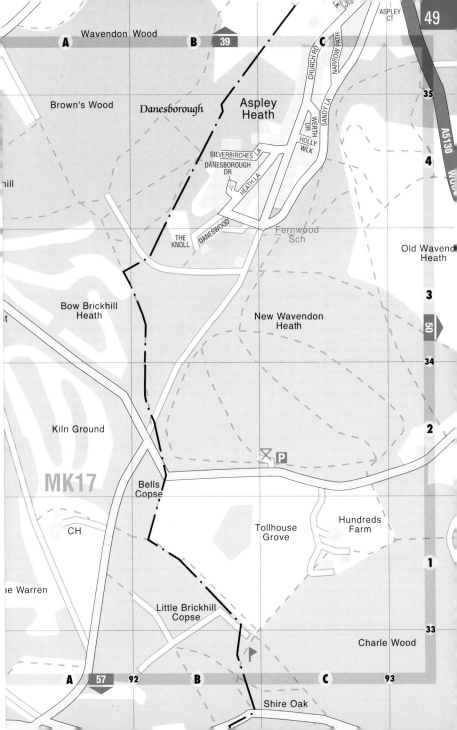

ASPLEY
CT

A

40

B

Aspley
Wood

C

NARROW PATH

SANDY LA

35

A5130

4

WOBURN RD

Mermaid's
Pond

ASPLEY LA

Old Wavendon
Heath

3

49

34

WOBURN RD

2

NEW

The Birch
(PH)

MK17

Dolton's
Farm

Hundreds
Farm

Horsemoor
Farm

1

Maryland
Coll

TIM

33

Charle Wood

LEIGHTON ST

93

A

B

94

C

Pinfold Pond

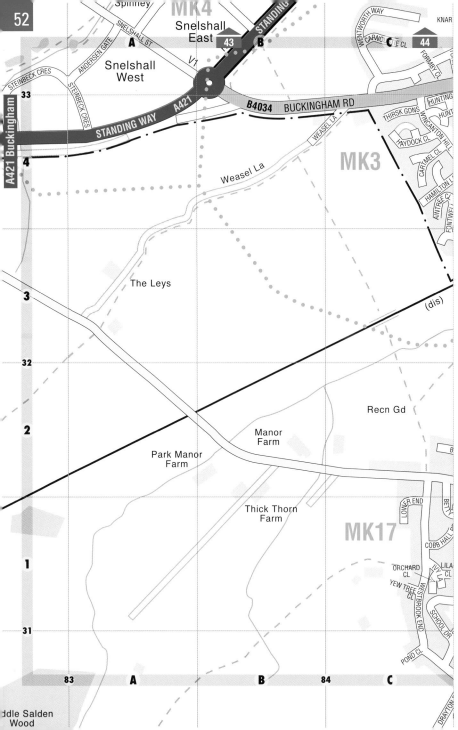

Spinney

MK4

Snelshall
East **43**

KNAR

WENTWORTH WAY

CARNO C TE CL

SNELSHALL ST

ANDERSEN GATE

Snelshall
West

V1

STANDING

FORMBY CL

STEINBECK CRES

33

A421 Buckingham

STEINBECK CRES

STANDING WAY A421

B4034 BUCKINGHAM RD

THIRSK GDNS

WINCANTON HILL

HUNTING

HUNT

HAYDOCK CL

4

Weasel La

WEASEL LA

CARTMEL CL

MK3

CARTMEL CL

HAMILTON L

AINTREE CL

FONTWEL

3

The Leys

(dis)

32

Recn Gd

2

Manor
Farm

Park Manor
Farm

B

LOWER END

BETT

COBB HALL

1

Thick Thorn
Farm

MK17

ORCHARD
CL

IVY LA

LILA
CL

YEW TREE
CL

WESTBROOK END

SCHOOL DR

31

POND CL

DRAYTON

ddle Salden
Wood

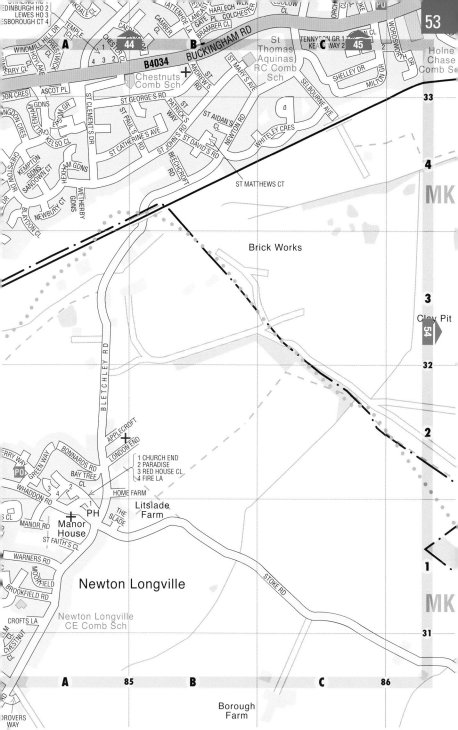

BUCKINGH

BURNS RD
MASEFIELD
RD
KIPLING
RD
CHAUCER
GR
BROWNING
CRES

TA Ctr

WELLIN
PL

P

WATER EATON RD

R.ST

NSET

WORDSWORTH DR

BYRON CL

SON GR 1
'S WAY 2

2

2

A

COTTINGHAM G

45

LBERT
CL

THY
CL

B

FRENSHAM
DR

BETTINA
GR

DOREEN
CL

BACCARA GR

FORD

C

46

W

Holne
Chase
Comb Sch

COLERIDGE
CL

CELINA CL

SHELLEY DR

MILTON GR

COLERIDGE
CL

Nature
Reserve

CORNELIA
CL

HUNTER DR

33

Bletchley

NE AVE

4

MK3

Blue
Lagoon

P

Bishop Parker
RC Comb
Sch

BARTON
RD

GIFFARD
RD

TIMMELL WAY

BALA WAY

Blue Lagoon
Park

TARBERT
CL

MENTEITH
CL

GARRY
CL

BRORA
CL

ENNELL GR

ALL
CL

DOON WAY

MAREE
CL

3

Clay Pit

53

DRAYTON RD

Leon Sch
&
Sports
Coll

32

2

Slad Farm

TULLA
CT

STRANGFORD DR

RU

Old Fox
Covert

1

Skew Bridge
Villa

MK17

31

86

A

B

87

C

Chadwell
Farm

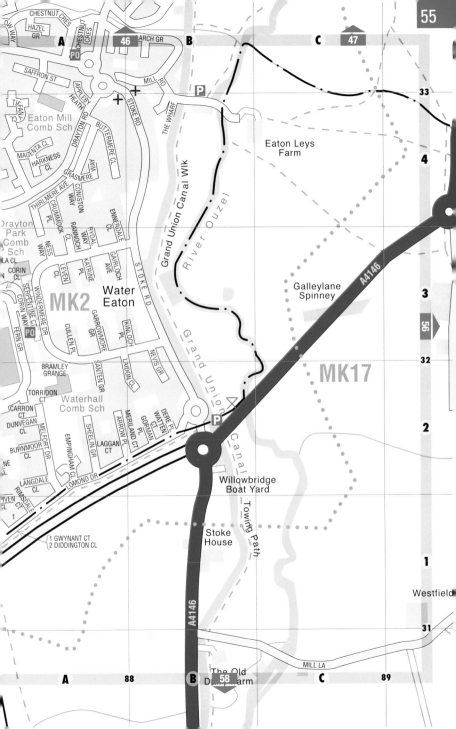

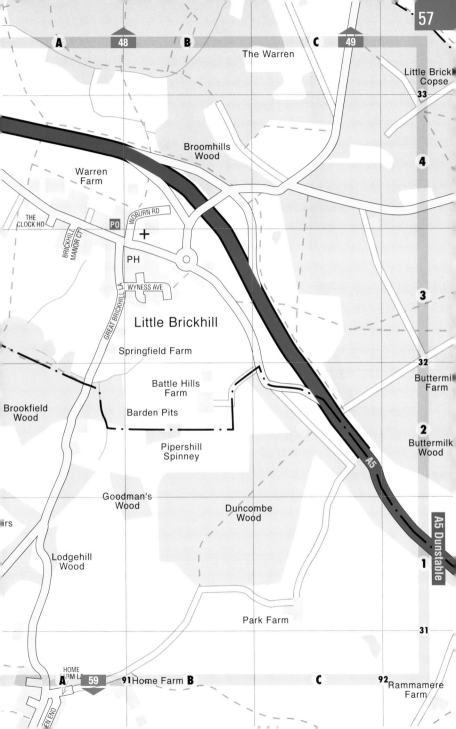

A | **48** | **B** | **C** | **49**

The Warren

Little Brick Copse

33

Broomhills Wood

4

Warren Farm

THE CLOCK HO

WOBURN RD

PO

BRICKHILL MANOR CT

PH

GREAT BRICKHILL LA

WYNESS AVE

Little Brickhill

3

Springfield Farm

32

Buttermi Farm

Battle Hills Farm

Brookfield Wood

Barden Pits

2

Buttermilk Wood

Pipershill Spinney

A5

Goodman's Wood

irs

Duncombe Wood

A5 Dunstable

Lodgehill Wood

1

Park Farm

31

HOME FARM LA

A | **59** | 91 Home Farm **B** | **C** | 92 Rammamere Farm

EN END

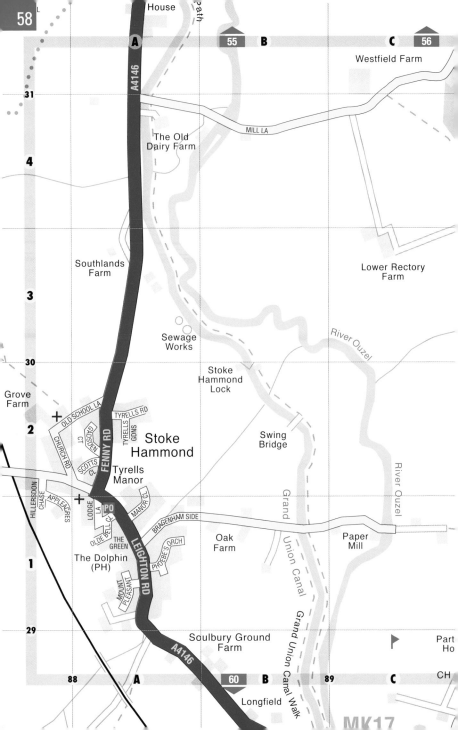

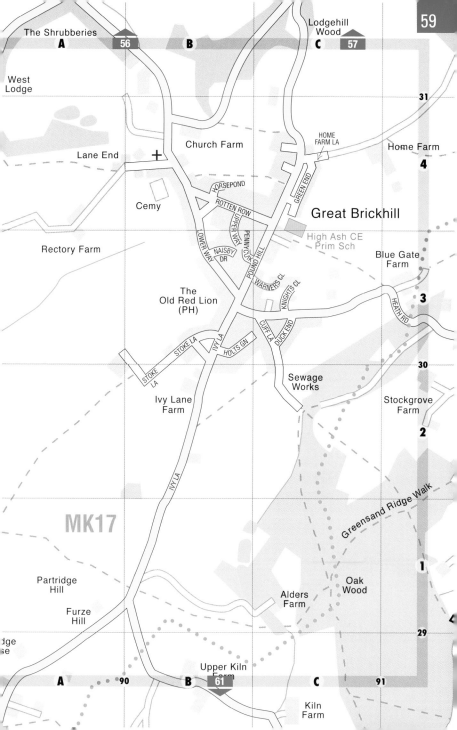

The Shrubberies

Lodgehill Wood

West Lodge

31

Church Farm

HOME FARM LA

Home Farm

4

Lane End

Green End

Great Brickhill

HORSEPOND

ROTTEN ROW

Cemy

UPPER WAY

PENNYCUIK

POUND HILL

High Ash CE Prim Sch

Blue Gate Farm

Rectory Farm

LOWER WAY

NAISBY DR

WARNERS CL

KNIGHTS CL

HEATH RD

3

The Old Red Lion (PH)

STOKE LA

IVY LA

HOLTS GN

CUFF LA

DUCK END

Sewage Works

30

STOKE LA

Ivy Lane Farm

Stockgrove Farm

2

IVY LA

MK17

Greensand Ridge Walk

1

Partridge Hill

Oak Wood

Furze Hill

Alders Farm

dge se

29

Upper Kiln Farm

Kiln Farm

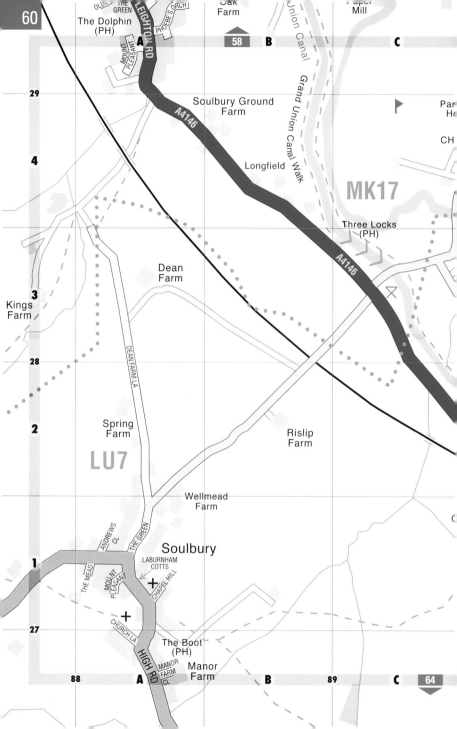

Oak
Wood

Visitor
Ctr

BRICKHILL RD

Stockgrove
Country Park

Baker's
Wood

Fox
Corner

A

B

C

29

Kingswood
Farm

iln
arm

4

REACH C

BAKERS WOOD CL

Shire
Oak

The
Grange

GRA

GRANGE CT

Rushmere
Park

St Leonard's
Heath And Reach
Lower Sch

THOMAS

THRIFT RD

WOODLAND CL

SHEEPC

PO CF

3

Recn
Gd

LINSLADE RD

SYLVESTER ST

BIRD

SEND

PINKLE HILL

61

EMU CL

CHANDLER
PL

THE OAKS

HEATH
GN

28

THE STILE

ABBEY WLK

LANE'S END

WELLING
HO

LU7

LINSLADE RD

Sewage
Works

Nar s Gadley
Farm

2

Rushmere

CRADDOCKS DR

Oak Bank
Sch

OAK BANK DR

CH

THE HEATH

HEATH CL

DUKES
RIDE

SANDY LA

PLANTATION RD

CARLTON GR

SANDY LA

HEATH PARK RD

HEATHWOOD

Grange
Mill

1

Greensand Ridge Walk

REDWOOD
GLADE

REDWOOD
GLADE

COPPER BEECH WAY

HEATH PARK
DR

HEATH RD

PINE CL

27

TALL
PINES

Dovery Down
Lower Sch

POPLAR CL

MANOR
CT
P

A

65

B

66

C

9

Old Linslade
Manor

92

Old
Linslade

OXENDON
CT

TAYLOR'S RIDE

ROBINSWOOD
CL

WOODL

AVE

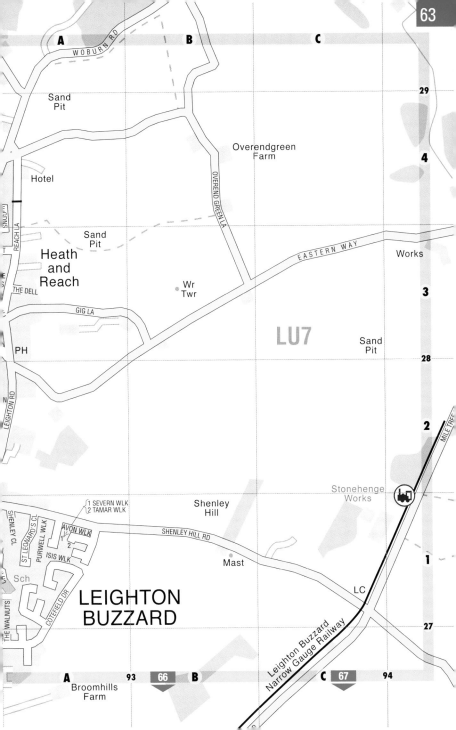

A WOBURN RD **B** **C**

29

Sand
Pit

Overendgreen
Farm

4

Hotel

OVEREND GREEN LA

Sand
Pit

EASTERN WAY

Works

Heath
and
Reach

THE DELL

Wr
Twr

3

GIG LA

LU7

Sand
Pit

PH

28

LEIGHTON RD

2

MILE TREE

Stonehenge
Works

1 SEVERN WLK
2 TAMAR WLK

Shenley
Hill

1

SHENLEY'S CL

ST LEONARD'S CL

PURWELL WLK

AVON WLK

SHENLEY HILL RD

ISIS WLK

Mast

Sch

LEIGHTON
BUZZARD

COTEFIELD DR

LC

THE WALNUTS

27

A 93 **66** **B** **C** **67** 94

Broomhills
Farm

Leighton Buzzard
Narrow Gauge Railway

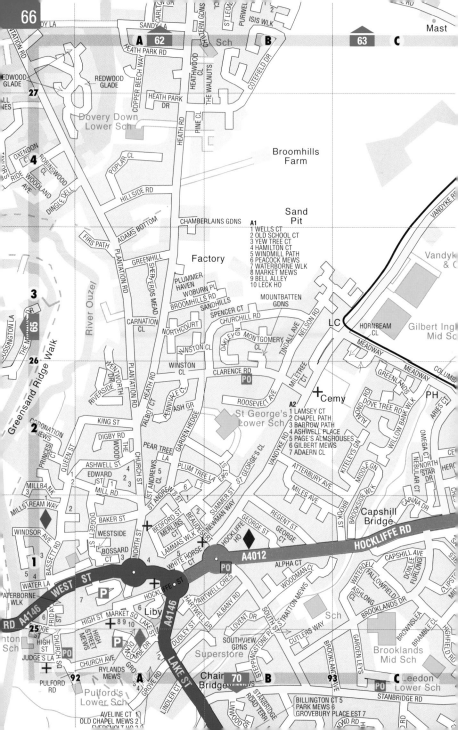

A 63

LC

Leighton Buzzard
Narrow Gauge Railway

27

4

Manor
Farm

Upper Sch
n Coll

LEIGHTON
BUZZARD

eld

Clipstone

Clipstone
Farm

3

26

Clipstone Brook

PHOENIX CL

HYDRUS DRI

PPENINE WAY

Beaudesert
Lower Sch

STURN CL

GEMINI CL

LYRA CL

SIRIUS

JUPITER DR

MERCURY WAY

BRIGGINGTON
COTTS

Model
Farm

2

ORION WAY

CYGNUS
DR

AQUILA RD

LEIGHTON RD

NEPTUNE GDNS

SIRIUS RD

BARLEYCORN
CL

RYE CL

Hill
Farm

A4012

A4012 Woburn

LC

OAKFIELD
GDNS

WHEATFIELD CL

MILLERS CL

2

1

3

4

1 THRESHERS CT
2 DRIVERS CT
3 TILLER CT
4 HARVESTER CT

LEIGHTON RD

DANES WAY

CL

VICTORIA
TERR

RUSSELL WAY

HINTON CL

MEADOW WAY

Leedon

CHERRYCOURT WAY
IND EST

Charity
Farm

1

SSWAY

MARLEY FIELDS

Young
Ind Est

CHERRYCOURT WAY

ACACIA CL

Ind
Est

ORCHARD EST

25

LC

A 94

B 71

C

95

EAVES

Commerce Way

LEIGHTON BUZZARD

Valley Farm

64

Rocklane Farm

25

4

3

24

2

Long Spinney

1

Waterloo Farm

LEIGHTON RD

Grimstone's Furze

Whitefields

Ascott Home Farm

A418 Aylesbury

23

A418

WELLA

Ascott

89

A

Round Spinney

B

90

C

Ascott House

DERWENT R

CALDER GDNS

CARRON CL

MAREE CL

NEVIS CL

LOMOND DR

DELAMERE GDNS

RANNOCK GDNS

BEWDLEY DR

BLAKEDOWN RD

ERIBOLL CL

MELFORT DR

MORAR CL

WINDERMERE GDNS

CONISTON RD

KENDAL GDN

ULLSWATER DR

CHELSEA

APPLE TREE VILLAGE EPSOM

LEVEN CL

Rock Lane

A418

A505

1 THRESHERS CT
2 DRIVERS CT
3 TILLER CT
4 HARVESTER CT

VICTORIA TERR

A

B

67

C

LEIGHTON RD

RUSSELL WAY

MEADOW WAY

Leedon

CHERRYCOURT WAY
IND EST

ORCHARD ES

Charity
Farm

HINTON CL

CROSSWAY

25

MARLEY FIELDS

Young
Ind Est

CHERRYCOURT WAY

ACACIA CL

4

Ind
Est

LC

GREAVES WAY

COMSIB CL

COMMERCE WAY

Commerce Way
Ind Est

LEAROYD WAY

ADASTRAL AVE

SWALES DR

CONCORD WAY

LEIGHTON WAY

ODELL WAY

HARMONY ROW

LEIGHTON RD

Midway

ROUNDEL DR

GIBSON DR

ESMONDE CL

RAF
Stanbridge

MANNOCK DR

NICHOLSON

3

HAWKER CL

TRENT WAY

MIDDLETON WAY

24

BYFORD WAY

MOORHOUSE PATH

BYFORD PATH

WOODHOUSE WAY

2

m

A505 Dunstable (A5)

A505

A505

1

Green
Farm

23

Mead
Open Farm &
Rare Breeds

HILL VIEW LA

GADDESDEN TURN

Billington

A

94

B

C

95

BILLINGTON RD

A4146 Hemel Hempstead

Walker's Farm

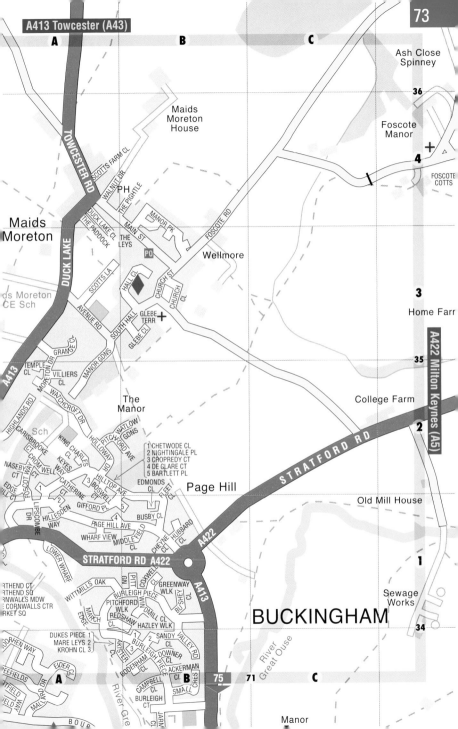

Index

Street names are listed alphabetically and show the locality, the Postcode district, the page number and a reference to the square in which the name falls on the map page

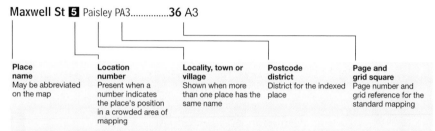

Maxwell St 5 Paisley PA3..............36 A3

Place name
May be abbreviated on the map

Location number
Present when a number indicates the place's position in a crowded area of mapping

Locality, town or village
Shown when more than one place has the same name

Postcode district
District for the indexed place

Page and grid square
Page number and grid reference for the standard mapping

Public and commercial buildings are highlighted in magenta. **Places of interest** are highlighted in blue with a star ★

Abbreviations used in the index

Acad	Academy	Ct	Court	Hts	Heights	Pl	Place
App	Approach	Ctr	Centre	Ind	Industrial	Prec	Precinct
Arc	Arcade	Ctry	Country	Inst	Institute	Prom	Promenade
Ave	Avenue	Cty	County	Int	International	Rd	Road
Bglw	Bungalow	Dr	Drive	Intc	Interchange	Recn	Recreation
Bldg	Building	Dro	Drove	Junc	Junction	Ret	Retail
Bsns, Bus	Business	Ed	Education	L	Leisure	Sh	Shopping
Bvd	Boulevard	Emb	Embankment	La	Lane	Sq	Square
Cath	Cathedral	Est	Estate	Liby	Library	St	Street
Cir	Circus	Ex	Exhibition	Mdw	Meadow	Sta	Station
Cl	Close	Gd	Ground	Meml	Memorial	Terr	Terrace
Cnr	Corner	Gdn	Garden	Mkt	Market	TH	Town Hall
Coll	College	Gn	Green	Mus	Museum	Univ	University
Com	Community	Gr	Grove	Orch	Orchard	Wk, Wlk	Walk
Comm	Common	H	Hall	Pal	Palace	Wr	Water
Cott	Cottage	Ho	House	Par	Parade	Yd	Yard
Cres	Crescent	Hospl	Hospital	Pas	Passage		
Cswy	Causeway	HQ	Headquarters	Pk	Park		

Index of localities, towns and villages

A

Aspley Guise 41 A2
Aspley Heath 49 B4
Atterbury 23 B2

B

Bancroft 19 A3
Beanhill 35 C2
Birchmoor Green 50 C2
Blakelands 12 A3
Bleak Hall 35 A3
Bletchley 45 B1
Bolbeck Pk 11 C1
Bourton 75 B4
Bow Brickhill 48 A3
Bradville 10 A1
Bradwell 19 B2
Bradwell Abbey 19 A1
Bradwell Common 19 C1
Bragenham 61 B4
Broughton 23 B1
Browns Wood 38 A2
Buckingham 72 C2

C

Caldecote 13 A3
Caldecotte 47 B4
Calverton 16 C1
Campbell Park 21 B1
Central Milton Keynes 27 A3
Chackmore 72 A4
Church End 41 C3
Clipstone 67 C3
Coffee Hall 27 C1
Conniburrow 20 C2
Cosgrove 6 C4
Crownhill 25 B1

D

Deanshanger 14 B2
Downhead Park 21 C3
Downs Barn 21 B3

E

Eaglestone 28 B1
Emerson Valley 43 C4

F

Far Bletchley 44 B1
Fenny Lock 46 C4
Fenny Stratford 46 B3
Fishermead 28 A3
Fox Milne 23 A2
Fullers Slade 17 B2
Furzton 34 B2

G

Giffard Park 11 C4
Granby 35 C1
Great Brickhill 59 C4
Great Holm 25 B2
Great Linford 11 A2
Greenleys 17 C3

H

Haversham 9 A4
Hazeley 32 B3
Heath and Reach 63 A3
Heelands 20 A2
Husborne Crawley 41 C2

K

Kents Hill 30 A1
Kiln Farm 17 C1
Kingston 30 C4
Knowlhill 34 B4

L

Leadenhall 28 A2
Leedon 67 A1
Leighton Buzzard 70 C3
Linslade 65 A1
Little Brickhill 57 B3
Loughton 26 A2

M

Maids Moreton 71 A4
Medbourne 32 C3
Middleton 22 C1
Milton Keynes 20 B3
Milton Keynes Village 29 B4
Monkston 30 A3
Monkston Park 29 B3
Mount Pleasant 74 C3

N

Neath Hill 21 A4
Netherfield 36 A4
New Bradwell 9 B2
Newport Pagnell 3 A3
Newton Longville 53 A1
Northfield 23 A3

O

Oakgrove 29 A4
Oakhill 32 B2
Oldbrook 27 B2
Old Farm Park 38 C3
Old Linslade 65 A4
Old Stratford 6 A1
Old Wolverton 8 C2
Oxley Park 32 C1

P

Page Hill 71 B2
Passenham 16 A2
Pennyland 21 B2
Pineham 13 A1

R

Redmoor 35 B2
Rooksley 26 B4
Rushmere 62 A2

S

Shenley Brook End 43 B4

Shenley Church End 32 C4
Shenley Lodge 34 A3
Shenley Wood 33 A2
Snelshall East 43 C1
Snelshall West 43 B1
Soulbury 60 A1
Springfield 28 B4
Stacey Bushes 18 C2
Stantonbury 10 C1
Stoke Hammond 58 A2
Stonebridge 9 B1

T

Tattenhoe 43 B2
The Green Milton Keynes 29 A2
Newport Pagnell 3 B1
Tickford End 4 B2
Tilbrook 38 A1
Tinkers Bridge 36 B4
Tongwell 12 B2
Two Mile Ash 25 A4

W

Walnut Tree 38 A4
Walton 37 A3
Walton Manor 37 B4
Walton Park 37 B2
Water Eaton 55 A3
Wavendon 31 B1
Wavendon Gate 38 B4
Westcroft 42 C4
Willen 12 C1
Willen Park 22 A4
Winterhill 27 A2
Woburn 51 A1
Woburn Sands 39 B3
Wolverton 18 A3
Wolverton Mill 17 B4
Woolstone 22 B1
Woughton on the Green . . . 29 A2
Woughton Park 36 C4
Wymbush 25 C4

A

Abbeydore Gr MK10 . . . . 29 C3
Abbeyhill Rdbt MK12 . . . . 18 C2
Abbey Rd
　Milton Keynes,Bradwell
　MK13 . . . . 19 B2
　Milton Keynes,Simpson MK6 . . 36 C3
Abbey's Comb Sch MK3 . . . . 45 B4
Abbey Terr MK16 . . . . 3 C2
Abbey Way MK13 . . . . 19 C4
Abbey Wlk LU7 . . . . 62 C2
Abbotsbury MK4 . . . . 42 C4
Abbots Cl MK13 . . . . 19 C4
Abbotsfield MK6 . . . . 28 B2
Aberdeen Cl MK3 . . . . 45 A4
Abraham Cl MK15 . . . . 22 A4
Acacia Cl LU7 . . . . 71 B4
Ackerman Ho MK18 . . . . 75 B4
Ackroyd Pl MK5 . . . . 33 C3
Acorn Ho MK9 . . . . 27 A4
Acorn Wlk MK9 . . . . 27 B4
Adaern Ct **7** LU7 . . . . 66 A2
Adams Bottom LU7 . . . . 66 A3
Adams Cl MK18 . . . . 72 B1
Adams Ct MK6 . . . . 28 C2
Adastral Ave LU7 . . . . 71 B4
Addington Rd MK18 . . . . 72 C1
Addington Terr MK18 . . . . . . 72 C1
Adelphi St MK9 . . . . 21 A2
Agora Ctr
　7 Milton Keynes MK2 . . . . . 46 A2
　Milton Keynes,Wolverton
　MK12 . . . . 8 C1
Ainsdale Cl MK3 . . . . 44 B3
Aintree Cl MK3 . . . . 52 C4
Akerman Cl MK12 . . . . 17 C3
Akister Cl MK18 . . . . 75 A4
Albany Cl MK14 . . . . 10 C1
Albany Rd LU7 . . . . 66 B1
Albert St MK2 . . . . 46 A2
Albion Pl MK9 . . . . 21 B1
Albury Ct **3** MK8 . . . . 25 C3
Aldenham MK6 . . . . 36 B3
Aldergill MK13 . . . . 20 A3
Aldermead MK12 . . . . 18 C3
Alderney Pl MK5 . . . . 33 A2
Aldrich Dr MK15 . . . . 13 A1
Aldwycks Cl MK5 . . . . 33 A4
Alexander Ho **1** MK2 . . . . . 46 A2
Alexandra Ct
　Leighton Buzzard LU7 . . . . 65 C2
　Milton Keynes MK13 . . . . 19 B2
Alexandra Dr MK16 . . . . 12 B4
Alladale Pl MK12 . . . . 18 B2
Allen Cl MK2 . . . . 54 C3
Allerford Ct MK4 . . . . 34 A2
Allington Circ MK4 . . . . 42 C3
Allison Cl MK15 . . . . 28 C3
All Saints View MK5 . . . . 26 B2
Almhouses MK14 . . . . 11 A3
Almond Cl MK16 . . . . 3 A1
Almond Rd LU7 . . . . 66 C2
Alpha Ct LU7 . . . . 66 B1
Alpine Croft MK5 . . . . 33 B1
Alston Dr MK13 . . . . 19 A1
Alstonefield **4** MK14 . . . . . 33 C1
Althorpe Cres MK13 . . . . 19 C4
Alton Gate MK4 . . . . 33 A1
Alverton MK14 . . . . 11 B2
Alwins Field LU7 . . . . 65 A2
Ambergate MK16 . . . . 23 C2
Amberley Wlk MK4 . . . . 42 C3
Ambridge Gr MK6 . . . . 28 C3
Ambrose Ct MK15 . . . . 28 C4
Amelias La MK9 . . . . 21 B1
Ames Cl MK6 . . . . 27 C2
Amherst Ct MK15 . . . . 12 B1
Amos Ct MK13 . . . . 19 B4
Ampleforth MK10 . . . . 30 A3
Ancell Rd MK11 . . . . 16 C3

Ancona Gdns MK5 . . . . 33 A1
Andersen Gate MK4 . . . . 43 B1
Andrewes Croft MK14 . . . . . . 11 B2
Andrews Cl LU7 . . . . 60 A1
Angel Cl MK15 . . . . 11 C1
Angelica Ct MK7 . . . . 37 B3
Anglesey Ct MK8 . . . . 26 A2
Angora Cl MK5 . . . . 33 B1
Angstrom Cl MK5 . . . . 33 C3
Angus Dr MK3 . . . . 45 A4
Annes Gr MK14 . . . . 10 C3
Annesley Rd MK16 . . . . 3 A1
Anson Rd MK12 . . . . 18 A4
Anthony Ct MK11 . . . . 16 B3
Appenine Way LU7 . . . . 67 A2
Appleby Heath MK2 . . . . 55 A4
Applecroft MK17 . . . . 53 A2
Appleton Mews **4** MK4 . . . 33 C1
Apple Tree Cl LU7 . . . . 69 A4
Appleyard Pl **1** MK6 . . . . . 27 B3
Approach The MK8 . . . . 25 B4
Aquila Rd LU7 . . . . 67 A2
Arbroath Cl MK3 . . . . 34 C1
Arbrook Ave MK13 . . . . 20 B1
Archers Wells MK3 . . . . 45 C4
Archford Croft MK4 . . . . 34 A1
Arden Park MK12 . . . . 8 A1
Ardley Mews MK10 . . . . 23 C1
Ardwell La MK12 . . . . 17 C3
Ardys Ct MK5 . . . . 26 B2
Argyll Ho MK3 . . . . 45 A3
Aris Way MK18 . . . . 74 C2
Arlington Ct MK4 . . . . 34 C1
Arlott Cres MK6 . . . . 27 C2
Armourer Dr MK14 . . . . 21 A4
Armstrong Cl MK8 . . . . 25 B1
Arncliffe Dr MK13 . . . . 19 C3
Arne La MK7 . . . . 38 B3
Arnold Cott MK19 . . . . 6 B1
Arrow Pl MK2 . . . . 55 A2
Arundel Gr MK3 . . . . 44 C1
Ascot Ct LU7 . . . . 69 A4
Ascot Ho MK9 . . . . 26 C4
Ascot Pl MK3 . . . . 44 C1
Ashbrook Fst Sch MK8 . . . . . 25 B3
Ashburnham Cl **2** MK3 . . . 44 B3
Ashburnham Cres LU7 . . . . . 69 B4
Ashby MK6 . . . . 28 A2
Ashdown Cl MK14 . . . . 11 C2
Ashfield Gr MK2 . . . . 46 A1
Ashfield MK14 . . . . 10 C2
Ashford Cres MK8 . . . . 32 B4
Ash Grange LU7 . . . . 70 B3
Ash Gr LU7 . . . . 66 A2
Ashlong Cl LU7 . . . . 66 C1
Ashpole Furlong MK5 . . . . . . 26 B1
Ashridge Cl MK3 . . . . 44 B1
Ashwell Place **4** LU7 . . . . . 66 A2
Ashwell St
　1 Leighton Buzzard LU7 . . . 65 C2
　Leighton Buzzard LU7 . . . . 66 A2
Ashwood MK13 . . . . 9 C1
Asplands Cl MK17 . . . . 39 C2
Aspley Ct MK17 . . . . 40 A1
Aspley Guise Lower Sch
　MK17 . . . . 41 A2
Aspley Guise Sta MK17 . . . . 40 B4
Aspley Hill MK17 . . . . 40 A2
Aspley La MK17 . . . . 50 C4
Astlethorpe MK8 . . . . 25 C4
Aston Cl MK5 . . . . 33 C3
Atherstone Ct MK8 . . . . 24 C4
Atkins Cl MK13 . . . . 19 C1
Atterbrook MK13 . . . . 19 B2
Atterbury Ave LU7 . . . . 66 B2
Attingham Hill MK8 . . . . 26 A3
Atwell Cl MK8 . . . . 25 B1
Auckland Pk MK1 . . . . 36 B2
Auden Cl MK16 . . . . 2 C3
Audley Mead MK13 . . . . 19 C1
Augustus Rd MK11 . . . . 16 C2
Austwick La MK4 . . . . 43 C4
Avant Bsns Ctr MK1 . . . . 46 A4

Avebury Bvd MK9 . . . . 27 B4
Avebury Rdbt MK9 . . . . 27 A3
Aveline Ct LU7 . . . . 70 A4
Avenue Rd MK18 . . . . 71 A3
Avery Ct MK16 . . . . 12 B4
Avington MK8 . . . . 25 B3
Avon Cl MK16 . . . . 3 C1
Avon Gr MK3 . . . . 44 C2
Avon Wlk LU7 . . . . 63 A1
Aylesbury St W MK12 . . . . . . 18 A4
Aylesbury St
　Milton Keynes,Bletchley
　MK2 . . . . 46 C2
　Milton Keynes,Wolverton
　MK12 . . . . 18 B4
Aylesford Gr MK10 . . . . 30 A3
Aynho Ct MK8 . . . . 25 C2
Ayrton Cl MK8 . . . . 32 B4
Ayr Way MK3 . . . . 44 C4

B

Babington Cl MK10 . . . . 23 B1
Baccara Gr MK2 . . . . 46 A1
Backleys MK7 . . . . 47 B4
Badgemore Ct MK8 . . . . 24 C4
Badgers Oak MK7 . . . . 30 B1
Badgers Way MK8 . . . . 75 A3
Badminton View MK8 . . . . . . 26 A3
Bagshot Ct MK2 . . . . 46 A1
Baily Ct MK5 . . . . 33 B3
Baisley Ho MK2 . . . . 46 B2
Baker St LU7 . . . . 66 A1
Bakers Wood Cl LU7 . . . . . . 62 C4
Bala Cl MK2 . . . . 55 A3
Bala Way MK2 . . . . 54 C3
Balcary Gr MK4 . . . . 43 A2
Baldwin Cres MK16 . . . . 3 B1
Balfe Mews MK7 . . . . 38 B2
Ball Moor MK18 . . . . 74 C2
Balmer Bridge MK18 . . . . 75 A1
Balmer Cut MK18 . . . . 75 A2
Balmerino Cl MK10 . . . . 30 B4
Balmoral Ct MK16 . . . . 3 A1
Balsam Cl MK7 . . . . 37 C4
Bampton Cl MK4 . . . . 44 C4
Banburies Cl MK3 . . . . 35 B1
Bancroft Rdbt MK13 . . . . 19 B3
Bank Court Mews MK12 . . . . . 8 C1
Bankfield Rdbt MK9 . . . . 28 A4
Banktop Pl MK4 . . . . 34 A1
Bantock Cl MK7 . . . . 38 A3
Barbers Mews MK14 . . . . 21 A4
Barbury Ct MK14 . . . . 11 C2
Bardsey Ct MK10 . . . . 30 A4
Barford MK11 . . . . 17 A2
Barham Lodge MK18 . . . . 74 B4
Barkers Croft MK12 . . . . 18 A2
Barkestone Cl MK4 . . . . 44 A3
Barleycorn Cl LU7 . . . . 67 A1
Barleycroft MK4 . . . . 34 C2
Barnabas Rd LU7 . . . . 69 A4
Barnes Pl MK6 . . . . 27 B2
Barnet Cl MK5 . . . . 32 B3
Barnfield Dr MK6 . . . . 36 A3
Barnsbury Gdns MK16 . . . . . . 3 B1
Barnsdale Dr MK4 . . . . 43 A4
Barnstable Ct MK4 . . . . 34 B1
Barons Cl MK2 . . . . 46 A2
Barrett Pl MK5 . . . . 33 A4
Barrington Mews **4** MK6 . . 27 B3
Barrow Path **3** LU7 . . . . . . 66 A2
Barry Ave MK14 . . . . 10 B1
Bartholomew Ct MK7 . . . . . . 37 B3
Bartlett Pl MK18 . . . . 71 A1
Barton Rd MK2 . . . . 54 C4
Bascote MK6 . . . . 36 B3
Basildon Ct
　1 Leighton Buzzard LU7 . . . 65 C1
　Milton Keynes MK8 . . . . 25 C2
Baskerfield Gr MK6 . . . . 28 C2
Bassett Ct MK16 . . . . 3 B2
Bassett Rd LU7 . . . . 65 C1
Bateman Croft MK5 . . . . 33 A4
Bates Cl MK15 . . . . 12 C1

Bath La MK18 . . . . 74 B1
Bath Lane Terr MK18 . . . . . . 74 B4
Baxter Cl MK8 . . . . 25 B1
Baynham Mead MK7 . . . . . . 30 B2
Bay Tree CI MK17 . . . . 53 A2
Beacon Ct MK4 . . . . 44 B4
Beaconsfield Pl MK16 . . . . . . 3 B2
Beadlemead MK6 . . . . 36 A4
Beales La MK7 . . . . 37 B3
Beanfare MK6 . . . . 35 C2
Beauchamp Cl MK14 . . . . . . 20 C4
Beaudesert LU7 . . . . 66 A1
Beaudesert Lower Sch LU7 . . 67 A2
Beaufort Dr MK15 . . . . 12 B1
Beaumaris Gr MK5 . . . . 33 B4
Beaverbrook Ct MK3 . . . . . . 45 B3
Beaver Cl MK18 . . . . 75 A3
Beckinsale Gr MK8 . . . . 25 B1
Bec La MK15 . . . . 12 A1
Beddoes Croft MK5 . . . . 32 C2
Bedford Rd MK17 . . . . 41 A3
Bedford St
　Leighton Buzzard LU7 . . . . 66 A1
　Milton Keynes,Bletchley MK2 . . 46 A2
　Milton Keynes,Wolverton
　MK12 . . . . 18 B4
　Woburn MK17 . . . . 51 A1
Bedgebury Pl MK7 . . . . 30 A2
Beech Cl MK18 . . . . 72 C2
Beechcroft Rd MK3 . . . . 53 B4
Beeches The
　Deanshanger MK19 . . . . 14 C1
　Milton Keynes MK1 . . . . 46 C3
Beech Fern MK7 . . . . 37 B3
Beech Gr LU7 . . . . 65 B1
Beech Rd MK16 . . . . 3 A1
Beech Tree Cl MK19 . . . . 8 C4
Beethoven Cl MK7 . . . . 38 C2
Beeward Cl MK12 . . . . 17 B3
Bekonscot Ct MK14 . . . . 11 B3
Bell Alley **9** LU7 . . . . 66 A1
Bellfounder Ho MK13 . . . . . . 19 C2
Bellini Cl MK7 . . . . 38 B3
Bellis Gr MK6 . . . . 28 C2
Bells Mdw MK15 . . . . 12 A1
Bellway MK17 . . . . 39 B4
Bellwether MK11 . . . . 17 B2
Belmont Cl MK8 . . . . 24 C4
Belsize Ave MK6 . . . . 28 B3
Belvedere La MK17 . . . . 47 A2
Belvedere Rdbt MK9 . . . . . . 21 A2
Belvoir Ave MK4 . . . . 44 A3
Benacre Croft MK4 . . . . 43 B2
Benbow Ct MK5 . . . . 26 A1
Bennet Cl MK11 . . . . 16 B2
Bentall Cl MK16 . . . . 12 B1
Benwell Cl MK13 . . . . 19 A3
Berberis Cl MK7 . . . . 37 B3
Bercham MK8 . . . . 25 B4
Beresford Cl MK4 . . . . 33 C1
Beretun MK8 . . . . 25 B3
Bereville Ct MK10 . . . . 22 C1
Berevilles La MK10 . . . . 22 C1
Bergamot Gdns MK7 . . . . . . 37 C3
Berkshire Ave MK5 . . . . 33 A1
Berling Rd MK8 . . . . 25 C4
Bernardines Way MK18 . . . . 75 A3
Bernay Gdns MK15 . . . . 12 A1
Bernstein Cl MK7 . . . . 38 A2
Berry La MK17 . . . . 41 A4
Berrystead MK7 . . . . 37 C1
Berry Way MK17 . . . . 53 A2
Bertram Cl MK13 . . . . 10 A2
Berwald Cl MK7 . . . . 38 B2
Berwick Dr MK3 . . . . 45 A4
Bessemer Ct MK14 . . . . 11 C3
Bettina Gr MK2 . . . . 46 A1
Betty's Cl MK17 . . . . 53 A1
Beverley Pl MK6 . . . . 28 B4
Bewcastle Row MK4 . . . . 42 C3
Bewdley Dr LU7 . . . . 64 C1
Bickleigh Cres MK4 . . . . 34 B1
Bideford Ct LU7 . . . . 64 C2
Bideford Cl MK4 . . . . 44 C2
Bignell Croft MK5 . . . . 26 B3

Bilbrook La MK4 . . . . 34 A2
Billington Ct LU7 . . . . 70 B4
Billingwell Pl MK6 . . . . 28 B4
Bilton Rd MK1 . . . . 46 B4
Bingham Cl MK4 . . . . 44 A3
Birchen Lee MK4 . . . . 44 A4
Birchfield Gr MK2 . . . . 46 A1
Birchmoor Gn MK17 . . . . 51 A2
Birdlip La MK7 . . . . 30 B1
Bird's Hill LU7 . . . . 62 C3
Birkdale Cl MK3 . . . . 44 B1
Bishop Cl LU7 . . . . 71 A4
Bishop Parker RC Comb Sch
  MK2 . . . . 54 C4
Bishops Cl MK18 . . . . 74 B3
Bishopstone MK13 . . . . 19 C3
Bishops Wlk MK17 . . . . 39 C1
Blackberry Ct MK7 . . . . 37 C4
Blackdown MK11 . . . . 17 A2
Blackham Ct MK6 . . . . 27 B1
Blackheath Cres MK13 . . . . 20 B1
Blackhill Dr MK12 . . . . 17 B4
Blackmoor Gate MK4 . . . . 44 C4
Blackthorn Gr MK17 . . . . 39 B2
Blackwell Pl MK5 . . . . 33 B2
Blackwood Cres MK13 . . . . 18 C4
Blairmont St MK9 . . . . 21 A2
Blakedown Rd LU7 . . . . 68 C4
Blakeney Ct MK4 . . . . 43 C2
Blanchland Circ MK10 . . . . 30 A3
Blansby Chase MK4 . . . . 34 A1
Blatherwick Ct MK5 . . . . 25 C1
Blaydon Cl MK3 . . . . 53 A4
Bleak Hall Rdbt MK6 . . . . 35 B3
Bleasdale MK13 . . . . 20 A3
Blenheim Ave MK11 . . . . 16 C2
Bletcham Rdbt MK1 . . . . 36 C1
Bletcham Way
  Milton Keynes MK1 . . . . 46 A4
  Milton Keynes MK1 . . . . 46 C4
  Walton Park MK7 . . . . 37 C2
Bletchley Com Hospl MK3 . . 45 B3
Bletchley Park Mus★ MK3 . . 45 B2
Bletchley Rd
  Milton Keynes MK5 . . . . 33 C2
  Newton Longville MK17 . . . . 53 A2
Bletchley Sta MK3 . . . . 45 C2
Blind Pond Ind Est MK17 . . 48 B4
Bliss Ct MK7 . . . . 38 A2
Blisworth MK6 . . . . 36 B3
Bluebell Cl MK18 . . . . 74 B3
Bluebell Croft MK7 . . . . 37 C4
Blundells Rd MK13 . . . . 20 A4
Blyth Ct MK4 . . . . 43 B2
Blythe Cl MK16 . . . . 3 C1
Bodenham Cl MK18 . . . . 75 B4
Bodiam Cl MK5 . . . . 33 B3
Bodle Cl MK15 . . . . 11 C1
Bodnant Ct MK4 . . . . 43 A4
Bolan Ct MK8 . . . . 32 C4
Bolton Cl MK3 . . . . 45 B4
Boltwood Gr MK5 . . . . 32 C3
Bond Ave MK1 . . . . 36 B1
Bone Hill MK18 . . . . 74 B3
Bonnards Rd MK17 . . . . 53 A2
Booker Ave MK13 . . . . 20 B2
Borodin Ct MK7 . . . . 38 B3
Borough Wlk MK9 . . . . 20 C1
Bossard Ct LU7 . . . . 66 A1
Bossiney Pl MK6 . . . . 27 C3
Bossington La LU7 . . . . 65 B1
Bostock Ct MK18 . . . . 74 B4
Boswell Ct MK18 . . . . 71 A2
Boswell La MK19 . . . . 14 C2
Bosworth Cl MK3 . . . . 44 C4
Bottesford Cl MK3 . . . . 44 B3
Boulevard The MK9 . . . . 27 B4
Boulters Lock MK14 . . . . 11 B4
Boundary Cres MK11 . . . . 16 C4
Boundary The MK6 . . . . 27 C2
Bounds Croft MK12 . . . . 18 A2
Bounty St MK13 . . . . 9 B1
Bourton Low MK7 . . . . 37 C3
Bourton Meadow Sch
  MK18 . . . . 75 B4

Bourton Rd MK18 . . . . 75 A4
Bourtonville MK18 . . . . 74 C4
Bow Brickhill CE Fst Sch
  MK17 . . . . 48 B4
Bow Brickhill Rd MK17 . . . . 39 A1
Bow Brickhill Sta MK7 . . . . 47 C4
Bowen Cl MK7 . . . . 38 A3
Bowes Cl MK16 . . . . 3 B1
Bowland Dr MK4 . . . . 43 C3
Bowles Pl MK6 . . . . 29 A1
Bowling Leys MK10 . . . . 30 A4
Bowl Rdbt The MK4 . . . . 34 B3
Boowood Ct 5 MK8 . . . . 25 C3
Bowyers Mews MK14 . . . . 21 A4
Boxberry Gdns MK7 . . . . 37 B4
Boxgrove Ct MK10 . . . . 30 A3
Boyce Cres MK7 . . . . 38 C3
Boycott Ave MK6 . . . . 27 B3
Brackley Rd MK18 . . . . 72 A1
Bradbourne Dr MK7 . . . . 38 A1
Bradbury Cl MK13 . . . . 19 B1
Bradfield Ave MK18 . . . . 72 C2
Bradford Gdns MK5 . . . . 33 C2
Bradley Gr MK4 . . . . 43 C4
Bradvue Cres MK13 . . . . 19 C4
Bradwell Common Bvd
  MK13 . . . . 20 A1
Bradwell Rd
  Milton Keynes,Bradville
  MK13 . . . . 19 B4
  Milton Keynes,Loughton MK5 . . 26 B2
  Milton Keynes MK5,MK8 . . . . 26 A3
Bradwell Village Mid Sch
  MK13 . . . . 19 C2
Bradwell Village Youth
  Hostel★ MK13 . . . . 19 B1
Braford Gdns MK5 . . . . 33 C2
Bragenham La LU7,MK17 . . 61 C3
Bragenham Side MK17 . . . . 58 B1
Brahms Cl MK7 . . . . 38 A3
Bramber Cl MK3 . . . . 44 C1
Bramble Ave MK14 . . . . 20 C2
Bramble Cl LU7 . . . . 66 C1
Bramley Grange MK2 . . . . 55 A2
Bramley Mdws MK16 . . . . 3 A1
Bramley Rd MK1 . . . . 36 B1
Brampton Ct MK13 . . . . 19 B4
Bransgill Ct MK13 . . . . 19 C2
Bransworth Ave MK10 . . . . 30 C2
Brantham Ct MK7 . . . . 37 B1
Braunston MK6 . . . . 36 B4
Braybrooke Dr MK4 . . . . 34 C2
Brayton Ct MK5 . . . . 34 A4
Breamore Ct MK8 . . . . 25 C2
Brearley Ave MK6 . . . . 27 B1
Breckland MK14 . . . . 20 B4
Brecon Ct MK10 . . . . 29 C3
Bremen Gr MK5 . . . . 33 B2
Brendon Ct MK4 . . . . 44 B4
Brent MK6 . . . . 36 B3
Bretby Chase MK4 . . . . 33 A1
Breton MK11 . . . . 16 C4
Brewster Cl MK5 . . . . 32 B3
Briar Hill MK12 . . . . 18 C2
Briar Lodge MK12 . . . . 18 B3
Briary View MK17 . . . . 42 A2
Brices Mdw MK5 . . . . 33 B1
Brick Cl MK11 . . . . 24 C4
Brickhill Manor Ct MK17 . . 57 A3
Brickhill St
  Giffard Park MK14 . . . . 11 C3
  Milton Keynes,Monkston Park
  MK10 . . . . 29 B4
  Milton Keynes,Willen Park
  MK15 . . . . 22 A4
  Walton Park MK7 . . . . 37 B2
Bridgeford Ct MK6 . . . . 27 B2
Bridge Rd MK19 . . . . 7 A4
Bridge St Buckingham MK18 . . 74 C4
  Leighton Buzzard LU7 . . . . 65 C1
  Milton Keynes MK13 . . . . 9 B1
Bridgeturn Ave MK12 . . . . 8 C2
Bridgewater Ho MK18 . . . . 74 B4
Bridgeway MK13 . . . . 9 C1
Bridge Wlk MK19 . . . . 14 C2

Bridgnorth Dr MK4 . . . . 42 C3
Bridle Cl MK13 . . . . 19 C4
Bridlington Cres MK10 . . . . 30 A3
Briggington Cotts LU7 . . . . 67 A2
Brill Pl MK13 . . . . 20 A1
Brindlebrook MK8 . . . . 25 B3
Brinkburn Chase MK10 . . . . 30 A3
Brinklow Rdbt MK10 . . . . 30 C3
Bristle Hill MK18 . . . . 74 B4
Bristow Cl MK2 . . . . 46 C3
Britten Gr MK7 . . . . 38 B3
Broad Arrow Ct MK14 . . . . 11 A1
Broad Dean MK6 . . . . 28 A2
Broadlands MK6 . . . . 36 A3
Broadpiece MK15 . . . . 11 C1
Broad Rush Gn LU7 . . . . 65 B2
Broad St MK16 . . . . 3 B2
Broadwater MK6 . . . . 36 B4
Broadway Ave MK14 . . . . 11 B4
Brockhampton MK15 . . . . 21 C4
Brockwell MK16 . . . . 3 B2
Bromham Mill MK14 . . . . 11 B4
Brooke Cl MK3 . . . . 45 A1
Brookfield La MK18 . . . . 74 C3
Brookfield Rd
  Haversham MK19 . . . . 8 C4
  Newton Longville MK17 . . . . 53 A1
Brooklands Ave LU7 . . . . 70 B4
Brooklands Dr LU7 . . . . 70 C4
Brooklands Mid Sch LU7 . . 70 C4
Brooklands Rd MK2 . . . . 46 A1
Brooks Ct MK18 . . . . 74 C4
Brookside Cl MK19 . . . . 15 C4
Brookside MK12 . . . . 18 B2
Brookside Wlk LU7 . . . . 66 C1
Brook St LU7 . . . . 66 C1
Brooksward Comb Sch
  MK14 . . . . 11 B1
Brookway MK19 . . . . 14 C2
Broomfield MK12 . . . . 18 B2
Broomhills Rd LU7 . . . . 66 A3
Broomlee MK13 . . . . 19 B3
Brora Cl MK2 . . . . 54 C3
Brough Cl MK5 . . . . 33 B3
Broughton Fields Comb Sch
  MK10,MK16 . . . . 23 C2
Broughton Manor Bsns Pk
  MK16 . . . . 23 C2
Brownbaker Ct MK14 . . . . 21 A4
Browne Willis Cl MK2 . . . . 46 B2
Browning Cl MK16 . . . . 2 C2
Browning Cres MK3 . . . . 45 B1
Brownset Dr MK4 . . . . 42 C3
Brownslea LU7 . . . . 66 C1
Browns Way MK17 . . . . 40 C3
Browns Wood Rdbt MK7 . . 38 A3
Broxbourne Cl MK14 . . . . 11 B4
Bruckner Gdns MK7 . . . . 38 B3
Brudenell Dr MK10 . . . . 30 C2
Brunel Ctr MK2 . . . . 46 A2
Brunleys MK11 . . . . 17 C1
Brushford Cl MK4 . . . . 34 B1
Bryony Pl MK14 . . . . 20 C3
Buckby MK6 . . . . 36 B4
Buckfast Ave MK3 . . . . 45 B4
Buckingham Cl MK16 . . . . 3 A1
Buckingham Gate MK6 . . . . 28 B3
Buckingham Hospl MK18 . . 72 C1
Buckingham Ind Pk MK18 . . 74 C2
Buckingham Prim Sch
  MK18 . . . . 71 A2
Buckingham Rd MK3 . . . . 44 B1
Buckingham Sch MK18 . . . . 74 C3
Buckingham Sq MK9 . . . . 26 C4
Buckingham St MK12 . . . . 8 C1
Buckland Dr MK6 . . . . 36 A4
Buckland Lodge MK6 . . . . 35 C4
Buckley Ct MK11 . . . . 17 A2
Buckman Cl MK12 . . . . 17 C3
Buckthorn MK12 . . . . 18 C3
Bull La MK2 . . . . 46 B2
Bulmer Cl MK10 . . . . 23 C1
Bunkers La LU7 . . . . 69 A4
Bunsen Pl MK5 . . . . 34 A2
Bunsty Ct MK11 . . . . 17 A3

Burano Cl MK7 . . . . 38 A4
Burchard Cres MK5 . . . . 33 B4
Burdeleys La MK5 . . . . 33 B2
Burdock Ct MK16 . . . . 2 B2
Burewelle MK8 . . . . 25 A3
Burgess Gdns MK16 . . . . 12 A4
Burghley Ct MK8 . . . . 25 C2
Burholme MK4 . . . . 34 A1
Burleigh Ct MK18 . . . . 75 B4
Burleigh Piece MK18 . . . . 71 B1
Burners La MK11 . . . . 17 C2
Burners Lane S MK11 . . . . 17 C1
Burnet MK14 . . . . 10 B1
Burnham Dr MK13 . . . . 20 A1
Burnmoor Cl MK2 . . . . 55 A2
Burns Cl MK16 . . . . 2 C2
Burns Rd MK3 . . . . 45 B1
Burrows Cl MK17 . . . . 39 C3
Burtree Cl MK12 . . . . 18 B3
Bury Ave MK16 . . . . 3 B2
Bury Cl MK16 . . . . 3 B2
Bury Lawn Sch MK14 . . . . 10 C1
Bury St MK16 . . . . 3 B2
Busby Cl MK18 . . . . 71 B1
Buscot Pl MK8 . . . . 25 C2
Bushey Bartrams MK5 . . . . 33 B1
Bushey Cl MK18 . . . . 71 B1
Bushfield Mid Sch MK12 . . 18 B4
Bushfields MK12 . . . . 18 B4
Bushy Cl MK3 . . . . 35 B1
Butcher La MK5 . . . . 33 A1
Bute Brae MK3 . . . . 44 C4
Butlers Gr MK14 . . . . 10 C2
Butterfield Cl MK15 . . . . 28 C4
Buttermere Cl MK2 . . . . 55 A4
Button Gr MK6 . . . . 28 A1
Buzzacott La MK4 . . . . 34 A1
Byerly Ho MK14 . . . . 21 A3
Byerly Pl MK14 . . . . 21 A3
Byford Path LU7 . . . . 71 A3
Byford Way LU7 . . . . 71 A3
Byrd Cres MK7 . . . . 38 B4
Byron Cl MK3 . . . . 45 A1
Byron Dr MK16 . . . . 2 C2
Byward Cl MK14 . . . . 11 A1

C

Cadeby Ct MK10 . . . . 23 C1
Cadman Sq MK5 . . . . 34 A3
Caernarvon Cres MK3 . . . . 44 C1
Caesars Cl MK13 . . . . 19 B3
Cairngorm Gate MK6 . . . . 27 C2
Caister Ct MK4 . . . . 42 C2
Caithness Ct MK3 . . . . 44 C4
Calamus Ct MK7 . . . . 37 C4
Caldecote La MK16 . . . . 13 B4
Caldecotte La MK7 . . . . 37 B1
Caldecotte Lake Dr MK7 . . 47 B4
Caldecotte Rdbt MK7 . . . . 37 A1
Calder Gdns LU7 . . . . 64 B1
Calder Vale MK3 . . . . 44 C3
Caldewell MK8 . . . . 25 A3
Caledonian Rd MK13 . . . . 9 A1
Calewen MK8 . . . . 25 B3
Calluna Dr MK3 . . . . 35 B1
Calvards Croft MK12 . . . . 18 A2
Calverleigh Cres MK4 . . . . 34 B1
Calverton La MK19 . . . . 24 B3
Calverton La Rdbt MK11 . . 24 B4
Calverton Rd MK11 . . . . 16 B2
Calves Cl MK5 . . . . 33 B1
Camber Cl MK3 . . . . 44 C1
Camberton Rd LU7 . . . . 69 B4
Cambridge St
  Milton Keynes,Bletchley
  MK2 . . . . 46 A2
  Milton Keynes,Wolverton
  MK12 . . . . 18 A4
Cambron MK8 . . . . 25 A4
Cam Ct MK3 . . . . 44 C2

Camlet Gr MK14 .... 10 C1
Camomile Ct MK7 .... 38 A3
Campania Cl MK10 .... 30 A4
Campbell Cl MK18 .... 75 B4
Campbell Park Rdbt MK9 .. 21 A1
Campion MK14 .... 11 A4
Canalside MK19 .... 6 B1
Canalside Rdbt MK9 .... 21 C2
Candlewicks MK7 .... 37 C4
Candy La MK5 .... 33 C2
Canon Harnett Ct MK12 ... 17 A4
Canons Rd MK12 .... 8 B1
Canons The MK16 .... 4 A1
Cantell Cl MK18 .... 72 C1
Cantle Ave MK14 .... 21 B3
Capel Dr MK14 .... 21 A3
Capian Wlk MK8 .... 25 B3
Capital Dr MK14 .... 20 C4
Capron MK5 .... 35 C3
Capshill Ave LU7 .... 66 C1
Caraway Cl MK7 .... 37 C2
Cardigan Ct MK3 .... 45 A3
Cardwell Cl MK4 .... 44 A4
Carhampton Ct MK4 ...... 34 B1
Carina Dr LU7 .... 66 C1
Carisbrooke Ct MK18 ..... 71 A2
Carisbrooke Way MK4 .... 42 C3
Carleton Gate MK15 ...... 13 A1
Carlina Pl MK14 .... 20 B1
Carlton Cl MK16 .... 4 A2
Carlton Gr LU7 .... 62 C1
Carlyle Ct MK16 .... 2 C2
Carnation Cl LU7 .... 66 A3
Carne The MK11 .... 16 C3
Carnot Cl MK5 .... 34 A2
Carnoustie Cl MK3 .... 44 A1
Carnweather Ct MK4 ..... 43 C2
Caroline Haslett Comb Sch
MK5 .... 33 C2
Carolus Creek MK15 ...... 11 C1
Carpenter Ct MK14 ...... 21 A4
Carrick Rd MK6 .... 27 C3
Carrington Rd MK16 ...... 3 A1
Carroll Cl MK16 .... 2 C3
Carron Cl LU7 .... 64 B1
Carron Ct MK2 .... 54 C2
Carteret Cl MK15 .... 13 A1
Carters La MK11 .... 17 B1
Cartmel Cl MK3 .... 52 C4
Cartwright Pl MK6 .... 27 B2
Carvers Mews MK14 ...... 21 A4
Cashmere Cl MK5 .... 33 B2
Casterton Cl MK13 .... 20 A2
Castle Acre MK10 .... 29 C3
Castle Cl MK18 .... 74 C4
Castle Ho 5 LU7 .... 65 B1
Castle Meadow Cl MK16 .. 4 A2
Castle Rose MK6 .... 36 B4
Castle St MK18 .... 74 C4
Castlesteads MK13 .... 19 A3
Caswell La LU7 .... 51 A1
Catchpole Cl MK12 ...... 17 C3
Catesby Croft MK5 ...... 26 C2
Cathay Cl MK3 .... 45 C1
Catherine Ct MK18 ...... 71 A2
Cavendish Cl MK5 .... 26 A1
Cavenham MK8 .... 25 C4
Cawardon MK4 .... 10 B1
Cawdor Rise MK4 .... 42 C4
Cawkwell Way MK2 ...... 46 A2
Caxton Rd MK12 .... 8 A1
Cecily Ct MK5 .... 33 B3
Cedar Lodge Dr MK18 ..... 8 C1
Cedars Comb Sch MK16 ... 3 B2
Cedars Upper Sch & Com Coll
The LU7 .... 69 B3
Cedars Way
  Leighton Buzzard LU7 ... 69 B3
  Newport Pagnell MK16 ... 3 B2
Celandine Ct MK7 .... 37 B3
Celina Ct MK2 .... 46 A1
Centauri Cl LU7 .... 66 C2

Centurion Ct MK11 .... 24 C4
Century Ave MK6 .... 27 B2
Cetus Cres LU7 .... 66 C1
Chackmore CE Sch MK18 .. 72 A4
Chadds La MK6 .... 28 C2
Chadwick Dr MK6 .... 28 B1
Chaffron Way
  Leadenhall MK6 .... 27 C1
  Milton Keynes,Oakgrove MK6,
  MK10,MK15 .... 29 A3
  Milton Keynes,Shenley Lodge MK4,
  MK5,MK6 .... 34 A3
Chalcot Pl MK8 .... 25 C2
Chalfont Ct MK13 .... 19 B4
Chalkdell Dr MK5 .... 33 A2
Challacombe MK4 .... 44 B4
Challenge Ho MK3 .... 45 C3
Chalmers Ave MK19 .... 8 C4
Chaloner Ct LU7 .... 70 B3
Chalwell Ridge MK5 ...... 33 C2
Chamberlains Gdns LU7 .. 66 A4
Champflower MK4 .... 34 B1
Chancery Ct MK13 .... 19 B4
Chandler Pl LU7 .... 62 C3
Chandlers Ct MK6 .... 36 C3
Chandos Cl MK18 .... 74 C3
Chandos Ct MK18 .... 74 C3
Chandos Pl MK2 .... 45 C2
Chandos Rd MK18 .... 74 C4
Channory Cl MK4 .... 43 B3
Chantry Cl MK17 .... 39 B4
Chapel Hill LU7 .... 60 A1
Chapel Path 2 LU7 ...... 66 A2
Chapel St MK17 .... 39 C2
Chaplin Gr MK8 .... 25 A1
Chapman Ave MK14 ...... 21 B4
Chapmans Dr MK19 .... 6 A1
Chapter Ho MK6 .... 35 B3
Chapter MK6 .... 35 B3
Charbray Cres MK5 ...... 33 B2
Chardacre MK8 .... 25 B3
Charles Way MK16 .... 3 B2
Charlewood Ho MK17 .... 39 C1
Charlock Ct MK16 .... 2 B2
Chartley Ct MK5 .... 33 C2
Chartmoor Rd LU7 ...... 70 A2
Chartwell Rd MK16 ...... 4 A2
Chase Ave MK7 .... 37 B2
Chatsworth MK8 .... 25 C4
Chaucer Cl MK16 .... 2 C2
Chaucer Rd MK3 .... 45 B1
Chawton Cres MK8 ...... 25 C3
Chelsea Gn LU7 .... 69 A4
Chelsea Ho 6 LU7 .... 65 B1
Cheltenham Gdns MK3 ... 53 A4
Cheneys Wlk MK3 .... 45 B4
Chepstow Dr MK3 .... 53 A4
Cheriton MK4 .... 34 C1
Cherleton MK8 .... 25 B3
Cherrycourt Way Ind Est
  LU7 .... 67 B1
Cherrycourt Way LU7 .... 71 A4
Cherry Rd MK16 .... 3 A1
Cherry Tree Wlk LU7 ..... 65 B1
Chervil MK7 .... 35 C3
Cherwell Ho MK3 .... 44 C2
Chesham Ave MK13 ...... 20 A1
Cheshire Rise MK3 .... 44 C3
Cheslyn Gdns MK14 ...... 11 C2
Chesney Wold MK6 ...... 35 A3
Chester Cl MK3 .... 44 B1
Chesterholm MK13 .... 19 A3
Chestnut Cl MK11 .... 16 B3
Chestnut Cotts MK18 .... 74 B3
Chestnut Cres MK2 ...... 46 B1
Chestnut Hill LU7 .... 65 A2
Chestnut Rise LU7 ...... 65 A2
Chestnuts Comb Sch MK3 . 44 C1
Chettle Pl NN12 .... 5 A4
Chetwode Ave MK10 ..... 30 B3
Chetwode Cl MK18 .... 71 A2
Chevalier Gr MK8 .... 25 A1
Cheviot Cl LU7 .... 64 C2
Cheyne Cl MK18 .... 71 B1
Chicheley St MK16 .... 4 A2

Chicksands Ave MK10 ..... 30 A4
Chievely Ct MK4 .... 44 A3
Childs Way MK4,MK5,MK6,
  MK10 .... 26 C1
Chillery Leys MK15 ...... 13 A1
Chillingham Ct MK5 ...... 33 B2
Chiltern Gdns LU7 .... 62 C1
Chilterns The LU7 .... 71 A4
Chiltern Trad Est LU7 .... 70 A3
Chingle Croft MK4 ...... 44 A4
Chippenham Dr MK10 .... 30 C3
Chipperfield Cl MK13 ..... 9 C1
Chipping Vale MK4 ...... 44 A4
Chirbury Ct MK10 .... 29 C3
Chislehampton MK15 .... 22 A1
Chiswick Ct MK4 .... 43 A4
Christchurch Gr MK12 ... 17 C4
Christian Ct MK15 ...... 12 C1
Christie Cl MK16 .... 2 C3
Christine Ho 3 MK2 ..... 46 A2
Church Ave MK4 .... 70 A4
Church Cl MK18 .... 71 B3
Church End Rd MK5 ...... 33 B2
Church End MK17 .... 53 A1
Church End MK17 .... 31 B1
Church Farm Cres MK14 .. 11 A2
Church Green Rd MK8 .... 45 B2
Church Hill
  Aspley Guise MK17 ...... 40 C3
  Milton Keynes MK8 ...... 25 C4
  Churchill Rd LU7 .... 66 B3
Church La
  Deanshanger MK19 ...... 14 C2
  Milton Keynes MK5 ...... 26 B2
  Walton MK7 .... 37 A4
Church Lees MK14 .... 10 C3
Church Pas MK16 .... 3 C2
Church Rd
  Aspley Heath MK17 ..... 39 C1
  Bow Brickhill MK17 ..... 48 B3
  Leighton Buzzard LU7 ... 69 B4
  Church Sq LU7 .... 69 C4
Church St
  Aspley Guise MK17 ..... 40 C3
  Buckingham MK18 ...... 74 B4
  Leighton Buzzard LU7 ... 66 A2
  Maids Moreton MK18 .... 71 B3
  Milton Keynes,Fenny Stratford
  MK2 .... 46 C3
  Milton Keynes,New Bradwell
  MK13 .... 9 B1
  Milton Keynes,Stony Stratford
  MK11 .... 16 B3
  Milton Keynes,Wolverton
  MK12 .... 8 C1
Church View Ct LU7 ..... 69 B4
Church View MK16 .... 3 C2
Church Wlk MK3 .... 45 A1
Cinnamon Gr MK7 .... 37 B3
Clailey Ct MK11 .... 17 A3
Clapham Pl MK13 .... 26 C4
Clare Croft MK10 .... 23 B1
Claremont Ave MK11 .... 16 C2
Clarence Ho MK9 .... 26 C4
Clarence Rd
  Leighton Buzzard LU7 ... 66 B2
  Milton Keynes MK11 .... 16 C3
Clarendon Dr MK8 ...... 25 C4
Claridge Dr MK10 .... 30 A4
Clarke Rd MK1 .... 36 B2
Clay Hill MK8 .... 25 B4
Clayton Gate MK14 ..... 11 C2
Cleavers Ave MK14 ..... 20 C1
Cleeve Cres MK3 .... 45 B4
Clegg Sq MK5 .... 33 C3
Clerkenwell Pl MK6 ..... 28 B4
Cleveland Dr LU7 .... 64 C2
Cleveland MK13 .... 19 C4
Clifford Ave MK2 .... 46 A1
Clifton Moor MK5 .... 32 B3
Cline Ct MK8 .... 32 C4
Clipstone Brook Lower Sch
  LU7 .... 66 B1
Clipstone Cres LU7 ...... 66 C1
Clock Ho The MK17 ..... 57 A4

Cloebury Paddock MK15 .. 22 A1
Close The
  Milton Keynes,Bradwell
  MK13 .... 19 B2
  Milton Keynes,The Green
  MK6 .... 29 A1
Cloudberry MK7 .... 37 B4
Cloutsham Cl MK4 .... 34 B1
Clover Cl MK5 .... 26 B2
Clover End MK18 .... 74 B3
Club Cotts MK17 .... 39 C2
Cluny Ct MK7 .... 38 B4
Clyde Pl MK3 .... 44 C3
Clydesdale Pl MK14 ..... 21 A2
Coachmaker Ct MK14 ... 21 A4
Cobb Hall Rd MK17 ..... 52 C1
Coberley Cl MK15 ...... 21 C4
Cobham Cl MK18 .... 72 B1
Cochran Cl MK8 .... 25 B1
Cockerell St MK5 .... 34 A3
Coffee Hall Rdbt MK6 ... 35 C4
Cofferidge Cl MK11 ..... 16 B3
Cogan Ct MK8 .... 25 B1
Coggeshall Gr MK7 ..... 30 C1
Coin Cl MK10 .... 23 A1
Colchester Ct MK3 ..... 44 C1
Colchester Wlk MK3 .... 44 C1
Coldeaton La MK4 ...... 33 C1
Cold Harbour CE Comb Sch
  MK3 .... 35 A1
Coleridge Cl
  Milton Keynes MK3 ..... 45 B1
  Newport Pagnell MK16 ... 2 B2
Colesbourne Dr MK15 ... 21 C4
Coleshill Pl MK13 ...... 20 A1
Colgrain St MK9 .... 21 B2
Colindale St MK9 ...... 29 B3
Colley Hill MK13 .... 19 B2
Collins Wlk MK16 .... 2 C2
Colne MK6 .... 36 B4
Colston Bassett MK4 .... 44 A3
Coltsfoot Pl MK14 ...... 20 B1
Colts Holm Rd MK12 ..... 8 B2
Columba Dr LU7 .... 66 C2
Columbia Pl MK9 .... 21 B1
Combe Martin MK4 ..... 34 B1
Comfrey Cl MK7 .... 37 B3
Commerce Way Ind Est
  LU7 .... 71 B4
Commerce Way LU7 ..... 71 B4
Common La
  Milton Keynes,Bradwell
  MK13 .... 19 B2
  Milton Keynes MK5 ..... 26 C2
Concord Way LU7 .... 71 B3
Concourse The 6 MK2 ... 46 A2
Concra Pk MK17 .... 40 A2
Condor Cl MK6 .... 28 A2
Congreve MK6 .... 36 B3
Coniston Rd LU7 .... 64 C1
Coniston Way MK2 ..... 55 A4
Conniburrow Bvd MK14 . 20 C2
Constable Cl MK14 ..... 11 B1
Constantine Way MK13 .. 19 A3
Conway Cl MK3 .... 45 A2
Conway Cres MK3 ...... 44 C2
Cook Cl MK7 .... 37 C2
Coopers Cl MK16 .... 3 B2
Coopers Mews MK14 .... 21 A4
Coots Cl MK18 .... 75 A3
Copeland Cl MK7 ...... 38 A3
Copes Haven MK5 ...... 33 C1
Copper Beech Way LU7 .. 62 C1
Coppin La MK13 .... 19 B1
Copthorne Pl MK7 ...... 30 B2
Corbet Ride LU7 .... 65 A2
Corbet Sq LU7 .... 65 A2
Corbett Cl MK15 ...... 12 C1
Cordwainer Ct MK14 ... 21 A4
Corfe Cres MK3 .... 45 A2
Coriander Ct MK7 ...... 37 C3
Corin Cl MK2 .... 55 A3
Corin Way MK2 .... 55 A3
Cork Pl MK3 .... 44 C4

Cornbury Cres MK15 . . . . 21 B4
Cornelia Cl MK2 . . . . 54 C4
Cornflower Pl MK18 . . . . 74 B3
Cornhill Cty Fst Sch MK6 . . 35 B4
Corn Hill MK8 . . . . 25 B3
Cornwall Gr MK3 . . . . 45 A3
Cornwalls Ctr The MK18 . . . 72 C1
Cornwalls Mdw MK18 . . . . . . 72 C1
Coronation Mews LU7 . . . . . . 65 C2
Coronation Rd MK11 . . . . 16 C3
Corrigan Cl MK3 . . . . 45 B2
Corsewall Pl MK4 . . . . 43 A3
Corsham Ct 4 MK8 . . . . 25 C3
Cosgrove Leisure Pk* MK19 . 7 B3
Cosgrove Rd MK19 . . . . 6 B1
Cosgrove Village Prim Sch
  MK19 . . . . 7 A4
Cosway Pl MK8 . . . . 32 B4
Cotefield Dr LU7 . . . . 63 A1
Cotman Cl MK12 . . . . 17 C3
Cotswold Dr LU7 . . . . 64 C2
Cottage Comm MK5 . . . . 26 B2
Cottesloe Ct MK11 . . . . 17 A3
Cottingham Gr MK3 . . . . 45 B1
Cottisford Cres MK14 . . . . . . 11 B3
Coulson Ave MK8,MK5 . . . . . . 32 C4
Countisbury MK4 . . . . 44 B4
Courteneys Lodge MK4 . . . . . 34 C1
Courthouse Mews MK16 . . . . . 3 B2
Courtlands LU7 . . . . 69 B4
Courtyard Arts Ctr* MK14 . . 11 A3
Coverack Pl MK4 . . . . 43 C2
Coverdale MK13 . . . . 20 A3
Cowdray Cl MK15 . . . . 22 A1
Cowper Cl MK16 . . . . 2 C2
Coxwell Cl MK18 . . . . 71 B1
Craddocks Cl MK13 . . . . 19 C1
Craddocks Dr LU7 . . . . 62 C1
Craigmore Ave MK3 . . . . 45 A2
Cranberry Cl MK7 . . . . 37 C4
Cranborne Ave
  Milton Keynes MK4 . . . . 42 C4
  Milton Keynes MK4 . . . . 43 A3
Cranbrook MK17 . . . . 39 C3
Crane Ct MK5 . . . . 26 B3
Cranesbill Pl MK14 . . . . 20 C2
Cranwell Cl MK5 . . . . 33 C1
Craven The MK13 . . . . 20 A2
Crawley Rd Woburn MK17 . . . 51 A2
  Woburn MK17 . . . . 51 B3
Creed St MK12 . . . . 8 C1
Creran Wlk LU7 . . . . 64 C1
Crescent The
  Haversham MK19 . . . . 9 A4
  Milton Keynes,Fenny Stratford
  MK2 . . . . 46 A3
  Milton Keynes,Giffard Park
  MK14 . . . . 11 A4
Creslow Ct MK11 . . . . 17 A3
Cressey Ave MK5 . . . . 33 C2
Cricket Green Rdbt MK9 . . . 21 C2
Cricklebeck MK13 . . . . 19 C3
Crispin Rd MK13 . . . . 10 A1
Crofts La MK17 . . . . 53 A1
Cromarty Ct MK3 . . . . 34 C1
Cromwell Ave MK16 . . . . 2 C1
Cromwell Ct MK18 . . . . 71 A2
Cropredy Ct MK18 . . . . 71 A2
Cropton Rise MK4 . . . . 43 B4
Cropwell Bishop MK4 . . . . . . 44 A3
Crosby Ct MK8 . . . . 32 C4
Cross End MK17 . . . . 31 C1
Crosshills MK11 . . . . 16 B2
Crosslands MK14 . . . . 11 A2
Crosslow Bank MK4 . . . . 34 A1
Cross St MK16 . . . . 3 B2
Crossway LU7 . . . . 67 A1
Crowborough La MK7 . . . . . . 30 A2
Crow La MK43 . . . . 41 C2
Crownhill Rdbt MK8 . . . . 25 B2
Crown Wlk MK9 . . . . 20 C1
Crowther Ct MK5 . . . . 34 A3
Croxley Ct 3 LU7 . . . . 65 C2
Croydon Cl MK4 . . . . 34 A1
Cruickshank Gr MK8 . . . . 25 B1

Crummock Pl MK2 . . . . 55 A4
Cuff La MK17 . . . . 59 C3
Culbertson La MK13 . . . . 18 C4
Cullen Pl MK2 . . . . 55 A3
Culmstock Cl MK4 . . . . 44 B4
Culrain Pl MK12 . . . . 18 B2
Culross Gr MK10 . . . . 30 A4
Cumbria Cl MK3 . . . . 45 A3
Currier Dr MK14 . . . . 21 A4
Curtis Croft MK5 . . . . 33 C1
Curzon Pl MK7 . . . . 38 C2
Cutlers Mews MK14 . . . . 21 A4
Cutlers Way LU7 . . . . 70 B4
Cygnus Dr LU7 . . . . 67 A2
Cypress MK16 . . . . 2 C1

D

Dalgin Pl MK9 . . . . 21 B1
Dalton Gate MK10 . . . . 23 A2
Dalvina Pl MK12 . . . . 18 B2
Danbury Ct MK14 . . . . 20 C3
Dandridge Ct MK8 . . . . 32 A4
Dane Rd MK1 . . . . 46 C4
Danesborough Dr MK17 . . . . 49 B4
Danesbrook Cl MK4 . . . . 34 B2
Danes Way LU7 . . . . 67 A1
Daneswood MK17 . . . . 49 B3
Daniels Welch MK6 . . . . 35 B4
Dansteed Way
  Milton Keynes,Bradwell
  Common MK8,MK13,MK14,
  MK15 . . . . 20 A2
  Milton Keynes,Crownhill MK8 . 25 A1
Darby Cl MK5 . . . . 33 C3
Darin Ct MK8 . . . . 25 C2
Darley Gate MK14 . . . . 21 B3
Darnel Cl MK6 . . . . 35 B3
Dart Cl MK16 . . . . 3 C2
Dartington Pl MK4 . . . . 43 A3
Darwin Cl MK5 . . . . 32 C3
Daubeney Gate MK5 . . . . 33 A4
Davenport Lea MK7 . . . . 38 C3
Davison Ct MK8 . . . . 32 B4
Davy Ave MK5 . . . . 34 B4
Dawson Rd MK1 . . . . 36 B1
Daylesford Ct MK15 . . . . 21 C3
Deacon Pl MK10 . . . . 23 A1
Dean Farm La LU7 . . . . 60 A2
Deanshanger Prim Sch
  MK19 . . . . 14 C1
Deanshanger Rd MK19 . . . . . 15 C4
Dean's Rd MK12 . . . . 8 B1
Debbs Ct MK11 . . . . 16 C3
Deben Cl MK16 . . . . 4 A1
De Clare Ct MK18 . . . . 71 A1
Deepdale MK13 . . . . 20 A3
Deerfern Cl MK14 . . . . 11 A3
Deerfield Cl MK18 . . . . 75 A3
Deer Wlk MK9 . . . . 21 A1
Deethe Cl MK17 . . . . 39 C4
Delamere Gdns LU7 . . . . 64 C1
Delaware Dr
  Milton Keynes MK15 . . . . 12 A2
  Tongwell MK15,MK16 . . . . 12 A3
Delius Cl MK7 . . . . 38 A2
Dell The LU7 . . . . 63 A3
Deltic Ave MK13 . . . . 26 B4
De Montfort Univ MK7 . . . . . 30 A1
Denbigh East Ind Est MK1 . . 46 B4
Denbigh Hall Dr MK3 . . . . . . 35 A1
Denbigh Hall Ind Est MK3 . . 35 A1
Denbigh Hall MK3 . . . . 35 A1
Denbigh Rd MK1 . . . . 45 C4
Denbigh Sch MK5 . . . . 33 B4
Denbigh Way MK2 . . . . 46 A4
Denbigh West Ind Est MK1 . . 45 C4
Denchworth Ct 2 MK4 . . . . . 44 A4
Dene Cl MK17 . . . . 40 A2
Denham Cl MK3 . . . . 44 B2
Denison Ct MK7 . . . . 38 B4
Denmark St MK2 . . . . 46 C2
Denmead MK8 . . . . 25 B4
Dere Pl MK2 . . . . 55 B2

Derwent Cl MK16 . . . . 3 C2
Derwent Dr MK3 . . . . 44 C2
Derwent Rd LU7 . . . . 64 B1
Develin Cl MK14 . . . . 11 B1
Devon Cl MK3 . . . . 45 A3
Dexter Ave MK6 . . . . 27 C2
Dexter Ho MK7 . . . . 27 C2
Dickens Dr MK19 . . . . 15 C4
Dickens Rd MK12 . . . . 8 B2
Diddington Cl MK2 . . . . 54 C1
Digby Croft MK10 . . . . 22 C1
Digby Rd LU7 . . . . 66 A2
Dingle Dell LU7 . . . . 65 C4
Diswell Brook Way MK19 . . . 14 C3
Dixie La MK7 . . . . 38 A4
Dodkin MK6 . . . . 35 C3
Dodman Gn MK4 . . . . 43 C2
Doggett St LU7 . . . . 66 A1
Dolben Ct MK15 . . . . 12 C2
Donlee Furlong LU7 . . . . 66 C1
Donnington MK13 . . . . 19 C4
Don The MK3 . . . . 44 B3
Doon Way MK2 . . . . 54 C3
Dorchester Ave MK3 . . . . 45 B4
Doreen Cl MK2 . . . . 46 A1
Dorking Pl MK5 . . . . 33 C2
Dormans Cl MK10 . . . . 30 A4
Dorney Pl MK13 . . . . 20 A1
Dorset Cl MK3 . . . . 45 A3
Dorton Cl MK8 . . . . 25 C3
Douglas Pl MK6 . . . . 27 B2
Doune Ho MK3 . . . . 45 A4
Dove Cl Buckingham MK18 . . 75 A3
  Newport Pagnell MK16 . . . . . . 3 C2
Dovecote Ct MK14 . . . . 11 A3
Dovecote Cotts MK5 . . . . 33 B2
Dovecote MK5 . . . . 3 B2
Dover Gate MK3 . . . . 45 A2
Dovery Down Lower Sch
  LU7 . . . . 66 A4
Dove Tree Rd LU7 . . . . 66 C2
Downdean MK6 . . . . 28 A2
Downderry Croft MK4 . . . . . . 43 C2
Downer Cl MK18 . . . . 75 B4
Downham Rd MK17 . . . . 40 A2
Downland MK8 . . . . 25 B4
Downley Ave MK13 . . . . 20 A1
Downs Barn Bvd MK14 . . . . . 21 A3
Downs Barn Fst Sch MK14 . . 21 A3
Downs Barn Rdbt MK14 . . . . 21 A3
Downs View MK17 . . . . 48 A4
Drakeloe Cl MK17 . . . . 51 A2
Drakes Mews MK8 . . . . 25 C1
Drakewell Rd MK17 . . . . 48 B3
Drayton Park Comb Sch
  MK2 . . . . 55 A3
Drayton Rd MK2 . . . . 54 C3
Drew Ct MK3 . . . . 35 B2
Drivers Ct LU7 . . . . 67 A1
Drovers Croft MK12 . . . . 17 C2
Drummond Hay MK15 . . . . . . 12 B1
Dryden Cl MK16 . . . . 2 C2
Duchess Gr MK7 . . . . 30 C1
Duck End MK17 . . . . 59 C3
Duck Lake Cl MK18 . . . . 71 A4
Duck Lake MK18 . . . . 71 A3
Duck La MK17 . . . . 51 A1
Duckworth Ct MK6 . . . . 27 B1
Dudley Hill MK5 . . . . 33 B4
Dudley St LU7 . . . . 70 A4
Dukes Dr MK2 . . . . 46 A3
Dukes Piece MK18 . . . . 75 B4
Dukes Ride LU7 . . . . 62 B1
Duke St MK17 . . . . 40 B2
Dulverton Ct LU7 . . . . 64 C2
Dulverton Dr MK4 . . . . 34 B1
Dulwich Ct MK16 . . . . 12 B4
Dumfries Cl MK3 . . . . 35 A1
Dunbar Cl MK3 . . . . 44 B2
Duncan Gr MK5 . . . . 33 A4
Dunchurch Dale MK7 . . . . . . 37 C3
Duncombe Dr LU7 . . . . 70 A4
Duncombe St MK2 . . . . 46 A1
Dungeness Ct MK4 . . . . 43 B3
Dunkery Beacon MK4 . . . . . . 34 B1

Dunnet Cl MK4 . . . . 43 B2
Dunsby Rd MK6 . . . . 35 B2
Dunster Ct MK4 . . . . 34 C1
Dunthorne Way MK8 . . . . 32 B4
Dunvedin Pl MK12 . . . . 18 B2
Dunvegan Cl MK2 . . . . 55 A2
Duparc Cl MK7 . . . . 38 A3
Durate MK7 . . . . 30 A2
Durham Ho 1 MK3 . . . . 45 A3
Durlston End MK4 . . . . 43 B2
Durrans Ct MK2 . . . . 46 C3
Durrans Ho MK2 . . . . 46 C3
Durrell Cl LU7 . . . . 65 B1
Dyersdale MK13 . . . . 20 A3
Dyers Mews MK14 . . . . 21 A4

E

Eaglestone Rdbt MK6 . . . . . . 28 A2
Eagle Wlk MK9 . . . . 21 A1
Ealing Chase MK10 . . . . 29 C2
Eardley Pl MK8 . . . . 32 B4
Earls Cl MK2 . . . . 46 A2
Earls Willow MK13 . . . . 9 C2
Easby Gr MK10 . . . . 30 A3
Eastbury Ct MK4 . . . . 44 B3
East Chapel MK4 . . . . 43 C2
East Dales MK13 . . . . 20 A3
Eastern Way LU7 . . . . 63 C3
East Green Cl MK5 . . . . 33 A4
East La MK7 . . . . 29 C1
Eastoke Pl MK4 . . . . 43 B2
East Spur MK1 . . . . 29 C1
East St LU7 . . . . 66 B2
East Wlk N MK9 . . . . 27 B4
East Wlk S MK9 . . . . 27 B4
Eaton Ave MK2 . . . . 46 B1
Eaton Mill Comb Sch MK2 . . 55 A4
Ebbsgrove MK5 . . . . 26 B3
Eddington Ct MK4 . . . . 44 B3
Eden Way LU7 . . . . 70 B3
Eden Wlk MK3 . . . . 44 C3
Edgecote MK8 . . . . 26 A2
Edge Hill Ct MK18 . . . . 71 A2
Edinburgh Ho MK3 . . . . 44 B1
Edison Sq MK5 . . . . 34 A3
Edmonds Cl MK18 . . . . 71 B1
Edmund Ct MK5 . . . . 25 C1
Edrich Ave MK6 . . . . 27 C2
Edstone Pl MK4 . . . . 34 A1
Edward St LU7 . . . . 66 A2
Edwin Cl MK17 . . . . 48 B4
Edy Ct MK5 . . . . 26 A3
Edzell Cres MK4 . . . . 42 C4
Eelbrook Ave MK13 . . . . 26 C4
Egerton Gate MK5 . . . . 33 C2
Egmont Ave MK11 . . . . 16 C2
Eider Cl MK18 . . . . 75 A4
Elder Gate
  Milton Keynes,Rooksley
  MK9 . . . . 26 C3
  Milton Keynes,Winterhill MK9 . 26 C2
Eleanor Cl MK17 . . . . 51 A1
Eleanor Wlk MK17 . . . . 51 A1
Elfords MK6 . . . . 35 B4
Elgar Gr MK7 . . . . 38 A2
Eliot Cl MK16 . . . . 2 B3
Ellenstow MK13 . . . . 19 B2
Ellerburn Pl MK4 . . . . 33 C1
Ellesborough Gr MK8 . . . . . . 18 B1
Ellisgill Ct MK13 . . . . 19 C2
Elm Dr MK19 . . . . 14 B3
Elmers Pk MK3 . . . . 45 B2
Elm Gr MK17 . . . . 39 C2
Elmhurst Cl MK4 . . . . 35 A2
Elmridge Ct MK4 . . . . 44 A4
Elm St MK18 . . . . 74 C4
Elms The
  Leighton Buzzard LU7 . . . . . . 65 B1
  Milton Keynes MK3 . . . . 45 A2
Elthorne Way MK16 . . . . 12 B4
Elton MK6 . . . . 29 A1

Embleton Way MK18 . . . . **74** B3
Emerald Gate MK15 . . . . **22** C3
Emerson Valley Sch MK4 . . . . **44** A4
Emerton Gdns MK11 . . . . **16** C3
Emmett Cl MK4 . . . . **44** A3
Empingham Cl MK2 . . . . **55** A2
Emu Cl LU7 . . . . **62** C3
Enfield Chase MK14 . . . . **20** B3
Engaine Dr MK5 . . . . **25** C1
Enmore Gate MK9 . . . . **21** B1
Enmore Rdbt MK9 . . . . **21** B1
Ennell Gr MK2 . . . . **54** C3
Ennerdale Cl MK2 . . . . **55** A4
Enterprise La MK9 . . . . **21** B1
Enterprise Way LU7 . . . . **70** A3
Epsom Cl LU7 . . . . **69** A4
Epsom Gr MK3 . . . . **53** A4
Eriboll Cl LU7 . . . . **68** B4
Erica Rd MK12 . . . . **18** C2
Eridge Gn MK7 . . . . **30** A2
Eskan Ct MK9 . . . . **21** C2
Eskdale Way MK10 . . . . **23** C1
Esk Way MK3 . . . . **44** C3
Esmonde Cl LU7 . . . . **71** A3
Essenden Ct MK11 . . . . **17** A3
Essex Cl MK3 . . . . **45** A3
Esther Ct MK13 . . . . **19** B4
Eston Ct MK13 . . . . **19** B3
Etheridge Ave MK10 . . . . **30** C2
Ethorpe MK8 . . . . **25** B3
Eton Cres MK12 . . . . **18** A4
Europa Bsns Pk MK10 . . . . . . **30** C4
Evans Gate MK6 . . . . **27** B2
Evelyn Pl MK13 . . . . **9** C1
Everglade MK6 . . . . **28** A2
Everley Cl MK4 . . . . **34** A1
Eversholt Ho LU7 . . . . **70** A4
Evesham Way MK5 . . . . **32** B3
Exbury La MK4 . . . . **43** A3
Exchange Ho MK9 . . . . **27** B4
Exebridge MK4 . . . . **34** A1
Exmoor Gate MK4 . . . . **44** C4
Eynsham Ct MK15 . . . . **28** C4

F

Fadmoor Pl **3** MK4 . . . . **33** C1
Fairfax MK13 . . . . **20** A4
Fairford Cres MK15 . . . . **21** C4
Fairways MK8 . . . . **24** C4
Fairways Rdbt MK8 . . . . **24** C4
Falaise MK15 . . . . **12** A1
Falcon Ave MK6 . . . . **28** B4
Falconhurst Comb Sch
   MK6 . . . . **28** B2
Fallowfield LU7 . . . . **66** C1
Falmouth Pl MK6 . . . . **27** C3
Faraday Dr MK5 . . . . **34** A3
Farinton MK8 . . . . **25** C4
Farjeon Ct MK7 . . . . **38** B2
Farmborough MK6 . . . . **36** A4
Farnell Ct MK5 . . . . **26** C2
Farnham Ct MK8 . . . . **25** C3
Farrier Pl MK14 . . . . **21** B3
Farthing Ent Ctr The MK6 . . **36** A4
Farthing Gr MK6 . . . . **36** A4
Faulkner's Way LU7 . . . . **65** B1
Favell Dr MK4 . . . . **35** A2
Featherstone Rd MK12 . . . . . . **17** B3
Fegans Ct MK11 . . . . **16** B4
Felbridge MK7 . . . . **30** A1
Fennel Dr MK14 . . . . **20** C2
Fenny House Tuition Service
   MK6 . . . . **35** B4
Fennymere MK8 . . . . **25** A3
Fenny Rd MK17 . . . . **58** A2
Fenny Stratford Sta MK1 . . . **46** C3
Fenton Ct MK8 . . . . **25** C2
Fernan Dell MK8 . . . . **25** A1
Fernborough Haven **4**
   MK4 . . . . **44** A4
Ferndale MK6 . . . . **28** B3

Fern Gr MK2 . . . . **55** A3
Fernwood Sch MK17 . . . . **49** C4
Field Ct MK5 . . . . **26** B2
Field La MK12 . . . . **17** C3
Field Wlk MK9 . . . . **21** A1
Fife Ct MK4 . . . . **43** B2
Fife Ho MK3 . . . . **45** A3
Finch Cl MK10 . . . . **23** A1
Finch Cres LU7 . . . . **69** B3
Findlay Way MK2 . . . . **46** A2
Fingle Dr MK13 . . . . **9** A1
Firbank Ct LU7 . . . . **70** B3
Firbank Way LU7 . . . . **70** A3
Fire La MK17 . . . . **53** A2
Firs Path LU7 . . . . **66** A3
First Ave MK1 . . . . **46** A3
Fishermead Bvd MK6 . . . . **28** A3
Fishers Field MK18 . . . . **74** B4
Fitzhamon Ct MK12 . . . . **17** B3
Flambard Cl MK15 . . . . **11** C1
Flaxbourne Ct MK7 . . . . **30** C1
Flaxley Gate MK10 . . . . **30** A4
Fleet Cl MK18 . . . . **71** B2
Fleet The MK6 . . . . **28** B4
Fleming Dr MK6 . . . . **35** C4
Fletchers Mews MK14 . . . . . . **21** A4
Flintergill Ct MK13 . . . . **19** C2
Flint Ho **7** MK3 . . . . **45** A3
Flitton Ct MK11 . . . . **17** A3
Flora Thompson Dr MK16 . . . **2** B4
Florin Cl MK15 . . . . **11** C1
Folly Rd MK19 . . . . **14** B2
Fontwell Dr MK3 . . . . **52** C4
Forbes Pl MK5 . . . . **32** C2
Forches Cl MK4 . . . . **44** B4
Fordcombe Lea MK7 . . . . **30** B2
Ford St MK18 . . . . **74** C4
Forest Rise MK6 . . . . **28** B2
Forfar Dr MK3 . . . . **45** A4
Formby Cl MK3 . . . . **44** A1
Forrabury Ave MK13 . . . . **20** A1
Fortescue Dr MK5 . . . . **33** C4
Forthill Pl MK5 . . . . **25** C1
Fortuna Ct MK7 . . . . **38** A4
Forum The MK14 . . . . **20** C3
Foscote Rd MK18 . . . . **71** B3
Foscot Way MK18 . . . . **71** A2
Fossey Cl MK5 . . . . **33** A1
Fosters La MK13 . . . . **19** B1
Founders Mews MK14 . . . . . . **21** A4
Fountaine Cl MK14 . . . . **11** A1
Fowler MK14 . . . . **10** B1
Foxcovert Rd MK5 . . . . **33** A2
Foxgate MK16 . . . . **3** A2
Foxglove Cl MK18 . . . . **74** B3
Foxglove Ct MK16 . . . . **2** B2
Foxgoles Cl MK19 . . . . **15** A3
Foxhunter Dr MK14 . . . . **20** C4
Foxley Pl MK5 . . . . **26** C2
Fox Milne Rdbt MK10 . . . . . . **21** A2
Foxton MK6 . . . . **36** B4
Fox Way MK18 . . . . **75** A3
Fraderica Cotts MK16 . . . . **3** B1
Framlingham Ct MK5 . . . . **33** B3
France Furlong MK14 . . . . **11** B2
Frances Ct LU7 . . . . **65** B1
Francis Ct MK5 . . . . **33** C4
Frank Atter Croft MK12 . . . . . **18** A3
Frank Howe Ct MK6 . . . . **28** A3
Franklins Croft MK12 . . . . **18** A3
Frankston Ave MK11 . . . . **16** C3
Frederick Smith Ct MK12 . . . . **18** B2
Freeman Cl MK12 . . . . **17** C3
Frensham Dr MK2 . . . . **46** A1
Friary Gdns MK16 . . . . **12** B4
Friday St LU7 . . . . **65** C1
Fripp Gdns MK8 . . . . **32** B4
Frithwood Cres MK7 . . . . **30** B1
Froxfield Ct MK4 . . . . **44** A3
Fryday St MK6 . . . . **27** B1
Fulbrook Mid Sch MK17 . . . . **39** C3
Fulmer St
   Milton Keynes,Emerson Valley
   MK4 . . . . **34** A1

Fulmer St continued
   Milton Keynes,Medbourne MK8,
   MK5 . . . . **32** C4
Fulwell Cl MK14 . . . . **11** A2
Fulwoods Dr MK6 . . . . **28** A2
Furness Cres MK3 . . . . **45** B3
Furtho Cl MK19 . . . . **6** A1
Fury Ct MK8 . . . . **25** C1
Furze Way MK12 . . . . **18** A4
Furzton Rdbt MK4 . . . . **34** A2
Fyfield Barrow MK7 . . . . **38** A4
Fyne Dr LU7 . . . . **64** C2

G

Gables The LU7 . . . . **69** B4
Gable Thorne MK7 . . . . **38** B4
Gabriel Cl MK7 . . . . **38** A3
Gaddesden Cres MK7 . . . . **38** A4
Gadsden Ct MK17 . . . . **58** A2
Gainsborough Cl MK8 . . . . . . **32** B4
Gairloch Ave MK2 . . . . **55** A3
Gallagher Cl MK8 . . . . **25** B2
Galley Hill MK11 . . . . **17** A3
Galley La MK17 . . . . **56** A2
Galloway Cl MK3 . . . . **44** C4
Ganton Cl MK3 . . . . **44** B3
Garamonde Dr MK8 . . . . **25** C4
Garbo Cl MK8 . . . . **25** A1
Garden Hedge LU7 . . . . **66** A2
Garden Leys LU7 . . . . **70** C4
Gardiner Ct MK13 . . . . **18** C4
Garland Ct MK8 . . . . **25** B2
Garland Way LU7 . . . . **71** A3
Garraways MK6 . . . . **35** B4
Garrick Wlk MK9 . . . . **21** A1
Garrowmore Gr MK2 . . . . **55** A3
Garry Cl MK2 . . . . **54** C3
Garston MK8 . . . . **25** C3
Garthwaite Cres MK5 . . . . . . **33** B2
Garwood Cres
   Milton Keynes MK8 . . . . **32** A4
   Milton Keynes MK8 . . . . **32** B4
Gaskin Ct MK14 . . . . **21** B3
Gatcombe MK8 . . . . **25** C3
Gatehouse Sch The MK14 . . **10** C1
Gatewick La MK7 . . . . **37** B1
Gawcott Fields MK18 . . . . **74** A3
Gawcott Rd MK18 . . . . **74** A2
Gayal Croft MK5 . . . . **33** C2
Gemini Cl LU7 . . . . **67** B2
George Ct LU7 . . . . **66** B1
George St
   Leighton Buzzard LU7 . . . . . **66** B1
   Milton Keynes MK2 . . . . **46** C3
   Woburn MK17 . . . . **51** A1
George Yd MK11 . . . . **16** B3
Gerard Cl MK13 . . . . **9** C1
Germander Park Fst Sch
   MK14 . . . . **20** B2
Germander Pl MK14 . . . . **20** B2
Gershwin Ct MK7 . . . . **38** A2
Gibbwin MK14 . . . . **11** A2
Gibson Dr LU7 . . . . **71** A3
Gibsons Gn MK13 . . . . **20** A2
Gibsons Green MK13 . . . . **20** A2
Giffard Park Comb Sch
   MK14 . . . . **11** C4
Giffard Park Rdbt MK14 . . . . **2** B1
Giffard Rd MK2 . . . . **54** C4
Gifford Gate MK14 . . . . **11** A1
Gifford Pl MK18 . . . . **71** A1
Gig La LU7 . . . . **63** A3
Gilbert Cl MK3 . . . . **45** C1
Gilbert Inglefield Mid Sch
   LU7 . . . . **66** C3
Gilbert Mews **6** LU7 . . . . **66** A2
Gilbert Scott Rd MK18 . . . . . . **72** C2
Gilders Mews MK14 . . . . **21** A4
Giles Brook Comb Sch
   MK4 . . . . **43** B1
Gillamoor Cl **2** MK4 . . . . **33** C1
Gisburn Cl MK13 . . . . **19** C3
Gladstone Cl MK16 . . . . **3** C1
Glamis Ho MK3 . . . . **44** C1

Glamorgan Cl MK3 . . . . **45** A3
Glastonbury Cl MK3 . . . . **45** B4
Glastonbury Thorn Fst Sch
   MK5 . . . . **33** C4
Glazier Dr MK14 . . . . **21** A4
Glebe Cl
   Maids Moreton MK18 . . . . . **71** B3
   Milton Keynes MK5 . . . . **26** A2
Glebe Rdbt MK9 . . . . **21** C2
Glebe Rd MK19 . . . . **14** C3
Glebe Terr MK18 . . . . **71** B3
Gledfield Pl MK12 . . . . **18** B2
Gleeman Cl MK12 . . . . **17** B3
Gleneagles Cl MK3 . . . . **44** B1
Glenstal Pl MK9 . . . . **21** B1
Glenwoods MK16 . . . . **3** B1
Globe La LU7 . . . . **65** B3
Gloucester Rd MK12 . . . . **18** B3
Glovers La MK13 . . . . **19** C2
Glyn Sq MK12 . . . . **8** C1
Glyn St MK13 . . . . **9** C1
Glynswood Rd MK18 . . . . **72** B1
Goathland Croft **2** MK4 . . . **43** C4
Goddards Croft MK12 . . . . **18** A3
Godrevy Gr MK4 . . . . **43** C2
Godwin Ct MK7 . . . . **30** C1
Golden Dr MK6 . . . . **28** B2
Golden Riddy LU7 . . . . **65** B2
Goldilocks MK7 . . . . **37** C4
Goldmark Ct MK7 . . . . **38** B3
Gold Oak Wlk MK9 . . . . **21** A1
Goldsmith Dr MK16 . . . . **2** B2
Golspie Croft MK12 . . . . **18** A2
Goodman Gdns MK6 . . . . **29** A2
Goodrich Gn MK4 . . . . **42** C2
Goodwick Gr MK4 . . . . **43** C2
Goodwood MK8 . . . . **25** C2
Goosemere MK19 . . . . **14** C2
Goran Ave MK11 . . . . **16** C2
Gordale MK13 . . . . **20** A3
Goring MK14 . . . . **10** B1
Gorman Pl MK2 . . . . **55** B2
Gorricks MK11 . . . . **16** B2
Goslington MK1 . . . . **46** A4
Goudhurst Ct MK7 . . . . **30** B1
Gowers Yd MK19 . . . . **6** A1
Grace Ave MK6 . . . . **27** B2
Grafham Ct MK14 . . . . **11** C2
Grafton Gate MK9 . . . . **26** C3
Grafton Park MK9 . . . . **27** A3
Grafton St
   Milton Keynes,Bradwell
   MK13 . . . . **19** C2
   Milton Keynes,Granby MK1 . **35** C1
   Milton Keynes,New Bradwell
   MK12,MK13,MK19 . . . . **9** A2
   Milton Keynes,Winterhill MK6 . **27** B1
Grampian Gate MK6 . . . . **27** B1
Gramwell MK5 . . . . **25** C1
Granby Ct MK1 . . . . **35** B1
Granby Ind Est MK1 . . . . **35** C1
Granby Rdbt MK1 . . . . **36** A1
Granes End MK14 . . . . **11** A2
Grange Cl
   Leighton Buzzard LU7 . . . . . **69** A4
   Maids Moreton MK18 . . . . . **71** A3
Grange Ct LU7 . . . . **62** C4
Grange Farm Rdbt MK8 . . . . . **25** A1
Grange Gdns LU7 . . . . **63** A4
Grange Rd MK3 . . . . **45** A1
Grangers Croft MK12 . . . . **18** A2
Grantham Ct MK5 . . . . **34** A3
Granville Sq MK15 . . . . **12** B1
Grasmere Way
   Leighton Buzzard LU7 . . . . . **65** A1
   Milton Keynes MK2 . . . . **55** A4
Grasscroft MK4 . . . . **34** C2
Grassington MK13 . . . . **19** B3
Gratton Ct MK4 . . . . **34** A1
Graveney Pl MK6 . . . . **28** B4
Great Brickhill La MK17 . . . . **57** A3
Greatchesters MK13 . . . . **19** A3
Great Denson MK6 . . . . **28** A2
Great Ground MK14 . . . . **11** A1
Greatheed Dell MK7 . . . . **38** B2

Great Linch MK10. . . . . .30 A4
Great Linford Comb Sch
  MK14. .11 A2
Great Linford Lakes Wildfowl
  Ctr★ MK14 . . . . .10 B4
Great Monks St
  Milton Keynes,Wolverton
  MK12. . . . . .18 A3
  Milton Keynes,Wymbush MK8 . .25 B4
Great Ormes MK4. . . . . .43 A2
Great Pasture MK14 . . . . .23 A1
Great Slade MK18. . . . . .74 C2
Greaves Way LU7 . . . . .71 A4
Green End MK17. . . . . .59 C4
Green Farm Rd MK16 . . . . 3 B2
Greenfield Rd MK16 . . . . 2 C2
Greenhill Cl MK5 . . . . .26 A2
Greenhill LU7 . . . . .66 A3
Green La Aspley Guise MK17 . .40 C2
  Milton Keynes MK12. . . . . .18 B4
Greenlands Cl MK16 . . . . 2 C1
Greenlands LU7 . . . . .66 C2
Green Lane Rdbt MK9. . . . . . .21 C3
Greenlaw Pl MK3 . . . . .35 B1
Greenleas Lower Sch LU7. . .64 C1
Greenleys Fst Sch MK12 . .18 A3
Greenleys La MK12 . . . . .18 A2
Greenleys Mid Sch MK12 . .18 A3
Greenleys Rdbt MK12 . . . . . .17 C4
Green Park Comb Sch MK16 . .3 A1
Green Park Dr MK16 . . . . 3 B1
Greenside Hill MK4 . . . . .43 C3
Green The Cosgrove MK19 . . . . .7 B4
  Deanshanger MK19 . . . . .14 C2
  Milton Keynes,Loughton MK5. . .26 A2
  Milton Keynes,The Green
  MK6. . . . . .28 C2
  Newport Pagnell MK16 . . . . 3 B2
  Soulbury LU7 . . . . .60 A1
  Stoke Hammond MK17. . . . . . . .58 A1
Green Way MK17 . . . . .53 A2
Greenways MK17 . . . . .48 A4
Greenway Wlk MK18 . . . . . . .71 B1
Greenwich Gdns MK16 . . . . . .12 B4
Gregories Dr MK7 . . . . .38 B4
Grenville Comb Sch MK18 . .74 C3
Grenville Rd MK18 . . . . .72 B1
Greyfriars Ct MK10. . . . . .30 B4
Greys The MK6. . . . . .28 C2
Greystonley ❶ MK4. . . . . . . .44 A4
Griffith Gate MK10. . . . . .23 B1
Griffith Gate Rdbt MK10. . . . .30 A4
Griffon Cl MK6 . . . . .28 A1
Grigby Rise MK6. . . . . .28 A1
Grimbold Ct MK15 . . . . .12 B1
Grizedale MK13. . . . . .19 C3
Groombridge MK7 . . . . .30 A1
Grosmont Cl ❶ MK4. . . . . . . .43 C4
Groundsel Cl MK7 . . . . .37 C4
Grove Ash MK1 . . . . .36 B1
Grovebury Place Est LU7. .70 A4
Grovebury Rd
  Leighton Buzzard LU7 . . . . .70 A2
  Leighton Buzzard LU7 . . . . .70 A3
Grovebury Road Ind Est
  LU7 .70 A3
Grove Ind Sch The MK5 . . . . .26 C1
Grove Pl LU7 . . . . .70 A4
Grove Rd LU7. . . . . .70 A4
Grovesbrook MK17 . . . . .48 B4
Grove The
  Milton Keynes,Bradwell
  MK13. . . . . .19 B2
  Milton Keynes,Rickley Park
  MK3. . . . . .45 B2
  Newport Pagnell MK16 . . . . 3 A1
Groveway Bow Brickhill MK7 . .30 B1
  Milton Keynes,Redmoor MK5. . .35 B1
  Milton Keynes,Simpson MK6 . . .36 B3
Guest Gdns MK13. . . . . .10 A2
Guildford Ave MK4. . . . . .42 C3
Guise Ct MK17. . . . . .41 A2
Gulliver's Land★ MK15 . . . . .22 A2
Gundale Ct MK4. . . . . .43 C4
Gunmaker Ct MK14 . . . . .21 A4

Gunver La MK4 . . . . .43 C2
Gurnards Ave MK6. . . . . .28 A4
Gurney Cl MK5 . . . . .26 A1
Gwynant Cl MK2. . . . . .54 C1
Gyosei International Sch UK
  MK15. . . . . .22 A3
Gypsy La MK17 . . . . .41 A1

H

Haberley Mead MK13 . . . . . . .19 C1
Haddington Cl MK3 . . . . .44 C4
Haddon MK8 . . . . .25 C2
Hadley Pl MK13. . . . . .20 A1
Hadrians Dr MK13 . . . . .19 B3
Hainault Ave MK14. . . . . .11 C3
Haithewaite MK8 . . . . .25 A3
Haldene MK8 . . . . .25 B4
Hale Ave MK11 . . . . .16 C3
Hall Cl Maids Moreton MK18. . .71 B3
  Old Stratford MK19 . . . . .15 C4
Halswell Pl MK10 . . . . .23 B1
Haltonchesters MK13 . . . . . . .19 A4
Haly Cl MK13 . . . . .19 C2
Hambleton Gr MK4 . . . . .43 C4
Hamburg Croft MK5 . . . . .33 C1
Hamilton Cl ❹ LU7 . . . . .66 A1
Hamilton La MK3 . . . . .52 C4
Hamlins MK6. . . . . .35 B4
Hammerwood Gate MK7. . . . .30 A1
Hammond Cres MK15. . . . . . .21 C4
Hampshire Cl MK4. . . . . .45 A4
Hampson Cl MK13 . . . . .19 B3
Hampstead Gate MK13. . . . . .20 A1
Hampton MK8 . . . . .26 A2
Handel Mead MK7 . . . . .38 C3
Hanmer Rd MK6. . . . . .36 C3
Hanover Ct
  Leighton Buzzard LU7. . . . . . . .65 A1
  Milton Keynes MK14. . . . . .10 C1
Hanscomb Cl MK15 . . . . .28 C4
Hansen Croft MK5 . . . . .33 C3
Harborne Ct MK8 . . . . .24 C4
Harby Cl MK4 . . . . .44 A3
Harcourt Cl LU7 . . . . .65 B1
Harcourt MK13 . . . . .19 B1
Harding Rd MK10 . . . . .30 C2
Hardwick Mews MK17 . . . . . .39 C1
Hardwick Pl MK17 . . . . .39 C2
Hardwick Rd MK17 . . . . .39 C2
Harebell Cl MK7 . . . . .37 C3
Hare Cl MK18. . . . . .75 A3
Hareden Croft MK4 . . . . .43 C4
Hargreaves Nook MK14. . . . . .12 A4
Harkness Cl MK2 . . . . .55 A4
Harlans Cl MK6. . . . . .28 B2
Harlech Pl MK3. . . . . .44 C1
Harlequin Pl MK5. . . . . .33 A1
Harle Stone Ct MK14 . . . . . . .11 C3
Harmill Ind Est LU7. . . . . .70 A3
Harmony Row MK4. . . . . .71 B3
Harnett Dr MK12. . . . . .17 A4
Harpers La MK14 . . . . .11 B2
Harrier Cl MK6 . . . . .28 A2
Harrier Dr MK6 . . . . .28 A2
Harrison Cl MK5 . . . . .34 B4
Harrowden MK13 . . . . .10 A1
Harrow Rd LU7 . . . . .70 B3
Hartdames MK5 . . . . .33 B1
Hartfield Cl MK7. . . . . .30 A1
Hartington Gr MK4 . . . . .33 C1
Hartland Ave MK4 . . . . .43 C2
Hartley MK4 . . . . .11 A2
Hartwell Cres LU7 . . . . .66 B1
Hartwell Gr LU7 . . . . .66 A1
Hartwort Cl MK7. . . . . .37 C3
Harvard Cl MK14. . . . . .11 B4
Harvester Cl MK12 . . . . .17 C3
Harvester Ct LU7 . . . . .67 A1
Harwood St MK13 . . . . 9 C1
Hasgill Ct MK13 . . . . .19 C2
Haslow Ct MK8 . . . . .18 C1
Hastings MK11 . . . . .16 C3
Hatchlands MK8 . . . . .25 C3
Hathaway Ct MK8. . . . . .25 B2

Hatton MK6 . . . . .36 B4
Haukbee Gdns MK5 . . . . .34 B3
Haversham Fst Sch MK19 . . . 9 A4
Haversham Rd MK19. . . . . 8 C3
Hawker Cl LU7 . . . . .71 A3
Hawkhurst Gate MK7 . . . . . . .29 C1
Hawkins Cl MK11 . . . . .16 B3
Hawkmoor Cl MK6. . . . . .28 B2
Hawkridge MK4 . . . . .34 C1
Hawkshead Dr MK4. . . . . .34 A1
Hawkwell Est MK19 . . . . 6 A1
Hawthorn Ave MK2 . . . . .46 C2
Hawthorne Cl LU7 . . . . .65 B2
Haydock Cl MK3 . . . . .52 C4
Hayes Rd MK19 . . . . .15 A3
Hayman Rise MK8 . . . . .32 B4
Haynes Cl MK17 . . . . .48 B4
Haythorp Cl MK15 . . . . .21 C4
Haywards Croft MK12. . . . . . .17 C3
Hazeley Sch MK8. . . . . .32 B4
Hazel Gr MK2. . . . . .46 B1
Hazelhurst ❼ MK4. . . . . .43 C4
Hazelwood MK14 . . . . .11 B2
Hazley Wlk MK18 . . . . .71 B1
Heaney Cl MK18 . . . . 2 C3
Hearne Pl MK6 . . . . .27 C2
Heath Cl MK17. . . . . .40 A1
Heath Ct LU7 . . . . .62 A1
Heather Cl MK18 . . . . .74 B3
Heathercroft MK14 . . . . .11 A1
Heathfield MK12. . . . . .18 C2
Heath Gn LU7 . . . . .62 C3
Heath La MK17 . . . . .49 B4
Heath Park Dr LU7. . . . . .66 A4
Heath Park Rd LU7 . . . . .62 C1
Heath Rd LU7 . . . . .66 A4
Heath The LU7. . . . . .62 A2
Heathwood Cl LU7 . . . . .62 C1
Heathwood Lower Sch LU7 .63 A1
Hedgerows The MK4. . . . . . . .34 C2
Hedges Cl MK5. . . . . .33 C4
Hedingham Ct MK5 . . . . .33 B3
Heelands Fst Sch MK13. . . .19 C2
Hele Ct MK7 . . . . .37 C1
Helford Pl MK6 . . . . .28 A3
Heligan Pl MK4 . . . . .43 A3
Helmsley Rise MK4 . . . . .42 C3
Helston Pl MK6 . . . . .27 C3
Hemingway Cl MK16 . . . . 2 B3
Henders MK11. . . . . .16 C3
Hendrix Dr MK8 . . . . .25 A1
Hengistbury La MK4 . . . . .43 B3
Hensman Gate MK10. . . . . . . .23 A2
Hepleswell MK8 . . . . .25 B3
Hercules Cl LU7 . . . . .66 C2
Herdman Cl MK12 . . . . .17 C3
Heron Lodge MK14 . . . . .20 A4
Heronsgate Fst Sch MK7. . . .37 C3
Heronsgate Mid Sch MK7. . .37 C3
Herriot Cl MK16 . . . . 2 C3
Hertford Pl MK3 . . . . .45 A4
Hetton Cl MK15 . . . . .20 A2
Hexham Gdns MK3 . . . . .53 A4
Heybridge Cres MK7 . . . . .37 C1
Heydon Ct MK13 . . . . 9 C1
Hidcote Dr MK4 . . . . .43 A3
Hide The MK6 . . . . .36 A4
Higgs Ct MK5. . . . . .26 A2
High Ash CE Prim Sch
  MK17. . . . . .59 C4
Highbury La MK9 . . . . .21 C1
Highcroft LU7 . . . . .70 C4
Highfield Cl
  Milton Keynes MK3. . . . . .45 C4
  Newport Pagnell MK16 . . . . 4 A2
Highfield Rd LU7 . . . . .70 C4
Highgate Over MK7. . . . . .37 C4
Highgrove Hill MK8 . . . . .25 C2
High Halden MK7. . . . . .30 B2
Highland Cl MK3 . . . . .35 A1
Highlands Rd MK18 . . . . .71 A2
Highley Gr MK10. . . . . .23 C1
Highmore Croft MK8. . . . . . . .32 B4
High Park Dr MK12 . . . . .17 B4
High St The MK8 . . . . .25 B3

High St Buckingham MK18 . . .72 C1
Deanshanger MK19 . . . . .14 C2
Leighton Buzzard LU7. . . . . . . .66 A1
Leighton Buzzard LU7. . . . . . . .69 C4
Milton Keynes,Great Linford
  MK14. . . . . .11 A3
Milton Keynes MK2. . . . . .46 C3
Milton Keynes, New Bradwell
  MK13. . . . . 9 C1
Milton Keynes,Stony Stratford
  MK11. . . . . .16 B4
Newport Pagnell MK16 . . . . 3 C2
High Street Mews LU7 . . . . . .70 A4
High St MK17. . . . . .39 C2
High Trees MK6. . . . . .28 B2
Highveer Croft MK4. . . . . .43 C3
High View MK19 . . . . .14 C3
Hilbre Ct MK4 . . . . .43 A3
Hillbeck Gr MK10 . . . . .22 C1
Hillcrest Cl MK5 . . . . .33 C4
Hillcrest Rise MK18 . . . . .75 A2
Hillcrest Way MK18 . . . . .75 A1
Hillesden Way MK18 . . . . .71 A1
Hilliard Dr MK13 . . . . .19 B1
Hills Cl MK14 . . . . .11 A1
Hillside Rd LU7 . . . . .66 A4
Hilltop Ave MK18 . . . . .71 A2
Hill View MK16. . . . . .2 C1
Hillway MK17 . . . . .39 B4
Hillyer Ct MK6. . . . . .28 C3
Himley Gn LU7 . . . . .69 A4
Hindemith Gdns MK7. . . . . . .38 B3
Hindhead Knoll MK7. . . . . . . .37 C4
Hinton Cl LU7 . . . . .67 A1
Hinton Ct MK3. . . . . .45 A3
Hoathly Mews MK7 . . . . .30 B2
Hobart Cres MK15 . . . . .12 A1
Hockliffe Brae MK7 . . . . .38 A3
Hockliffe Ho LU7 . . . . .66 B1
Hockliffe Rd LU7 . . . . .66 C1
Hockliffe St LU7 . . . . .66 A1
Hodder La MK4. . . . . .44 A4
Hodge Lea La MK12. . . . . .18 B2
Hodgemoor Ct MK14. . . . . . . .11 B4
Hogarths Ct ❾ MK8 . . . . .25 C3
Holborn Cres MK4 . . . . .43 B2
Holdom Ave MK1 . . . . .46 B4
Holland Way MK16. . . . . 3 B1
Holliday Cl MK8 . . . . .25 B1
Hollies Ct LU7 . . . . .65 B1
Hollin La MK12 . . . . .18 C2
Hollinwell Cl ❸ MK4. . . . . . . .44 B3
Hollister Chase MK5 . . . . .33 C2
Holloway Dr MK18 . . . . .71 A2
Holly Cl MK8 . . . . .32 C4
Holly Wlk MK17. . . . . .49 C4
Holmewood MK4 . . . . .34 C2
Holmfield Cl MK6. . . . . .36 B3
Holm Gate MK5. . . . . .26 A2
Holmwood Fst Sch MK8 . . .25 C3
Holne Chase Comb Sch
  MK3. . . . . .45 B1
Holst Cres MK7 . . . . .38 B2
Holt Gr MK5 . . . . .26 A2
Holton Hill MK4 . . . . .44 A4
Holton Rd MK18 . . . . .72 C2
Holts Gn MK17. . . . . .59 B3
Holt The MK18 . . . . .75 A3
Holyhead Cres MK3. . . . . .44 A2
Holyrood MK8 . . . . .25 B2
Holy Thorn La MK5. . . . . .33 B3
Holywell Pl MK6 . . . . .28 C4
Home Cl MK3. . . . . .45 C4
Home Ct MK10 . . . . .23 B1
Home Farm La MK17. . . . . . . .59 C4
Home Farm MK17 . . . . .53 A2
Home Field MK7. . . . . .37 C1
Homeground MK18 . . . . .75 A2
Homeridings Ho MK13 . . . . . .19 C2
Homestall MK18 . . . . .74 C2
Homestall Ct MK16 . . . . .26 A1
Homestead The MK5 . . . . .33 B4

Homeward Ct MK5. . . . . 26 B1
Honey Hill Dr MK19. . . . . 14 C3
Honeypot Cl MK13. . . . . 19 C2
Honiton Ct MK7 . . . . 30 C1
Hooke The MK15. . . . . 12 C1
Hooper Gate MK15. . . . . 12 B1
Hopkins Cl MK10. . . . . 30 A4
Hoppers Mdw MK5 . . . . 26 A2
Hopton Gr MK16 . . . . 4 B1
Hornbeam Cl LU7. . . . . 66 C2
Hornbeam MK16. . . . . 2 C1
Hornby Chase MK4. . . . . 43 C4
Horners Croft MK12 . . . . 18 A3
Horn La MK11. . . . . 16 B3
Horsefair Gn MK11 . . . . 16 B3
Horsepond MK17 . . . . 59 B4
Horsepool La
  Aspley Guise MK17. . . . . 41 A2
  Husborne Crawley MK43 . . . . 41 B1
Horton Gate MK14 . . . . 11 B4
Horwood Cl MK1. . . . . 46 B4
Hospital Rdbt MK6. . . . . 35 C4
Houghton Ct **4** MK8. . . . . . . 25 C2
Housman Cl MK16 . . . . 2 C3
Howard Way MK16. . . . . 4 C1
Howe Ct MK10. . . . . 23 B1
Howe Park Fst Sch MK4. . . . . 43 C3
Howe Rock Pl MK4 . . . . 43 C3
Howitt Dr MK13. . . . . 10 A2
Howland Pl MK17. . . . . 51 A1
Hoylake Cl MK3. . . . . 44 B1
Hoyton Gate MK8. . . . . 32 B4
Hubbard Cl MK18 . . . . 71 B1
Huckleberry Cl MK7 . . . . 37 C4
Hudson La MK8. . . . . 25 A1
Hugh Park Cl MK5 . . . . 26 C2
Humber Way MK3 . . . . 44 C3
Hungerford Ho **1** MK4. . . . 44 B3
Hunsdon Ct MK14. . . . . 20 B4
Hunstanton Way MK3 . . . . 44 B2
Hunter Dr MK2 . . . . 54 C4
Hunters Reach MK13 . . . . 19 B1
Hunter St MK18. . . . . 74 B4
Huntingbrooke **6** MK8 . . . 25 C2
Huntingdon Cres MK3 . . . . . . 53 A4
Huntley Cres MK9 . . . . 21 B1
Huntsman Gr MK14 . . . . 11 C4
Hurley Croft MK10 . . . . 30 B3
Hurlstone Gr MK4 . . . . 34 B1
Husborne Crawley Lower Sch
  MK43. 41 C2
Hutchings Cl MK5 . . . . 26 A2
Hutton Ave MK6. . . . . 27 C3
Hutton Ct MK17. . . . . 39 C3
Hutton Way MK17. . . . . 39 C3
Huxley Cl MK16. . . . . 2 B2
Hyde Cl MK16 . . . . 12 B4
Hydrus Dr LU7. . . . . 67 A2
Hythe The MK8 . . . . 18 C1

I

Ibstone Ave MK13. . . . . 20 B2
Icknield Ho LU7. . . . . 70 A4
Illingworth Pl MK6. . . . . 27 C2
Ingleton Cl MK13 . . . . 20 A2
Innes Ct MK8 . . . . 32 B4
Innholder Ct MK14. . . . . 21 A4
Inverness Cl MK3 . . . . 45 A4
Ireland Cl MK7 . . . . 38 B2
Ironmonger Ct MK14. . . . . . . 21 A4
Irving Dale MK7. . . . . 38 C3
Isaacson Dr MK5 . . . . 26 B3
Isis Wlk Leighton Buzzard LU7. 63 A1
  Milton Keynes MK3. . . . . 44 C3
Isling Brook MK5 . . . . 33 C1
Iver Cl MK18. . . . . 74 B3
Ivester Ct LU7 . . . . 69 B4
Ivy Cl MK16. . . . . 4 A2
Ivy La Great Brickhill MK17 . . 59 B2
  Newton Longville MK17 . . . . 52 C1

J

Jacobs Cl MK14 . . . . 10 C1
Jamaica MK6. . . . . 35 B4
James Way MK1. . . . . 45 C3
Japonica La MK15 . . . . 22 A4
Jarman Ct MK18. . . . . 75 B4
Jeeves Cl MK6. . . . . 28 C1
Jenkins Cl MK5. . . . . 33 A3
Jenna Way MK16 . . . . 4 C1
Jennings MK14 . . . . 10 B1
Jerrard Cl LU7. . . . . 70 C4
Jersey Rd MK12 . . . . 18 A4
Johnston Pl MK6. . . . . 27 B2
Jonathans Ct MK6. . . . . 35 B4
Jonathans MK6. . . . . 35 B4
Joplin Cl MK8. . . . . 25 C1
Joules Ct MK5 . . . . 34 A3
Jubilee Terr MK11 . . . . 16 C3
Judge's La LU7 . . . . 69 C4
Juniper Gdns MK7. . . . . 30 B1
Jupiter Dr LU7 . . . . 67 A2

K

Kalman Gdns MK7 . . . . 38 B3
Kaplan Cl MK5. . . . . 33 C3
Katherine Ct MK7. . . . . 37 B2
Katrine Pl MK2 . . . . 55 A3
Keasden Ct MK4 . . . . 43 C4
Keaton Cl MK8. . . . . 25 A1
Keats Cl MK16 . . . . 2 C2
Keats Way MK3 . . . . 45 A1
Kellan Dr MK6. . . . . 28 A3
Keller Ct MK11. . . . . 24 B4
Kelsey Cl MK4 . . . . 43 A2
Kelso Cl MK3 . . . . 53 A4
Kelvin Dr MK5 . . . . 34 B4
Kemble Ct MK15 . . . . 21 C4
Kempton Gdns MK3. . . . . 53 A4
Kenchester MK13 . . . . 19 A3
Kendal Gdns LU7 . . . . 64 C1
Kendall Pl MK5. . . . . 32 C3
Kenilworth Dr MK3 . . . . 44 C2
Kennet Dr MK3 . . . . 44 C2
Kennet Pl MK3 . . . . 45 A2
Kennington Cl MK16 . . . . 3 B1
Kensington Dr
  Great Holm MK8. . . . . 26 A2
  Milton Keynes MK8. . . . . 25 C3
Kent Ho MK3 . . . . 45 A4
Kents Hill Fst Sch MK7 . . . . . 30 A1
Kents Hill Rdbt MK10 . . . . . . 29 C2
Kents Rd MK14. . . . . 10 C2
Kenwell Ct MK15 . . . . 22 A1
Kenwood Gate MK6. . . . . 28 B4
Keppel Ave MK19 . . . . 8 C4
Kepwick MK8. . . . . 25 B3
Kercroft MK8. . . . . 25 B4
Kernow Cres MK6. . . . . 28 A3
Kerria Pl MK3 . . . . 35 B1
Kersey MK14 . . . . 10 B2
Kestrel Way MK18 . . . . 75 B3
Ketelbey Nook MK7. . . . . 38 C3
Ketton Ct MK15 . . . . 12 C1
Kew Ct MK8 . . . . 25 C3
Keyes Way MK18. . . . . 71 A2
Keynes Cl MK16 . . . . 4 A2
Khasiaberry MK7 . . . . 37 C3
Kidd Cl MK8. . . . . 32 C4
Kidderminster Wlk MK10 . . 30 B4
Kildonan Pl MK12. . . . . 18 B2
Kilgour Ct **2** LU7. . . . . 65 C1
Kilkenny Ho MK4 . . . . 42 C4
Killerton Cl MK4. . . . . 43 A4
Kiln Farm Ind Est MK11. . . . . 17 C1
Kiln Farm Rdbt MK11 . . . . . . 17 B1
Kilwinning Dr MK10 . . . . 29 C3
Kimbolton Ct MK14 . . . . 11 C2
Kincardine Dr MK3. . . . . 35 A1
Kindermann Ct MK5. . . . . 33 C3
Kindleton MK14 . . . . 11 B2
King Charles Cl MK18. . . . . . 71 A2
King Edward St MK13. . . . . 9 B1
Kingfisher Ctr The MK16 . . . . 3 B1

Kingfisher Rd MK18. . . . . 75 B3
King George Cres MK11. . . . 16 C4
Kingsbridge MK4 . . . . 44 B4
Kingsbrook Sch MK19 . . . . . . 15 A2
Kingsfold MK13. . . . . 10 A1
Kingshill Dr MK19 . . . . 14 C3
Kingsley Cl MK16. . . . . 2 B2
Kingsmead Rdbt MK4. . . . . . 43 A2
Kingsoe Leys MK10 . . . . 30 A4
King St Leighton Buzzard LU7. 66 A2
  Milton Keynes MK11. . . . . . . 16 C4
Kingston Ave MK11 . . . . 16 C3
Kingston Rdbt MK10 . . . . 31 A3
Kinloch Pl MK2. . . . . 55 B3
Kinnear Ct MK8. . . . . 25 B1
Kinross Dr MK3. . . . . 44 C4
Kipling Dr MK16. . . . . 2 B2
Kipling Rd MK3. . . . . 45 B1
Kirkeby Cl MK14 . . . . 20 B4
Kirke Cl MK5 . . . . 33 B3
Kirkham Ct MK5. . . . . 26 C2
Kirkstall Pl MK6. . . . . 27 A2
Kirkwood Gr MK5. . . . . 32 B3
Kirtlington MK15 . . . . 21 C3
Kite Hill MK6. . . . . 28 B2
Kiteleys Gn LU7. . . . . 66 C2
Knapp Gate MK5. . . . . 25 C1
Knaresborough Ct MK3 . . . . 44 B1
Knaves Hill LU7. . . . . 65 A2
Knebworth Gate MK14. . . . . 11 C3
Knights Ct MK17 . . . . 59 C3
Knoll The MK17. . . . . 49 B3
Knowles Fst Sch MK2. . . . . . . 46 B2
Knowles Gn MK2 . . . . 46 A2
Knowles Mid Sch MK2. . . . . . 46 B2
Knowl Gate MK5. . . . . 26 C1
Knowlhill Rdbt MK5. . . . . 34 A4
Knox Bridge MK7. . . . . 30 B2
Kramer Ct MK8. . . . . 32 B4
Krohn Cl MK18. . . . . 75 B4
Krypton Cl MK5. . . . . 34 A4

L

Laburnham Cotts LU7. . . . . . 60 A1
Laburnum Gr MK2 . . . . 46 C1
Lacy Dr MK15. . . . . 11 C2
Ladymeadow Ct MK10 . . . . . 22 C1
Laggan Ct MK2 . . . . 55 A2
Lagonda Cl MK16. . . . . 4 A2
Laidon Ct MK2. . . . . 55 A2
Laker Ct MK6. . . . . 27 B1
Lakes La MK16. . . . . 3 A3
Lake St LU7 . . . . 70 A4
Lamb Cl MK16. . . . . 2 C2
Lamberhurst Gr MK7. . . . . . . 30 A2
Lamberts Croft MK12 . . . . . . 18 A3
Lamb La MK7. . . . . 30 C1
Lambourn Ct MK4 . . . . 44 B4
Lammas MK5 . . . . 35 B3
Lammas Wlk LU7 . . . . 66 A1
Lampitts Cross MK6 . . . . 35 C4
Lamport Ct MK8. . . . . 26 A2
Lamsey Ct **1** LU7. . . . . 66 A2
Lamva Ct MK11 . . . . 17 A3
Lanark Ho MK3 . . . . 45 A3
Lancaster Gate MK3 . . . . 44 C1
Landrace Ct MK5. . . . . 33 A1
Landsborough Gate MK15. . 12 B1
Lands End Gr MK4. . . . . 43 A2
Lanercost Cres MK10 . . . . 30 B3
Lane's End LU7. . . . . 62 C2
Lanfranc Gdns MK15. . . . . . . 12 A1
Langcliffe Dr MK13 . . . . 20 A3
Langdale Cl MK2 . . . . 55 A2
Langerstone La MK4. . . . . 43 C3
Langford Pl MK7. . . . . 37 B1
Langland Comb Sch MK4 . . . 34 A4
Langland Ho MK6. . . . . 36 A4
Langland Rd MK6. . . . . 36 A4
Langmuir Ct MK5. . . . . 34 A2
Langney Gn MK4 . . . . 43 B2
Langport Cres MK5 . . . . 32 B3
Langton Dr MK8 . . . . 18 C1
Lanner Wlk MK6. . . . . 28 B2

Lanthorn Cl MK14 . . . . 20 C4
Larch Gr MK2. . . . . 46 C1
Lark Cl MK18 . . . . 75 A3
Larkin Ct MK16 . . . . 2 C3
Larkspur Ave MK14 . . . . 20 C3
Larwood Pl MK6. . . . . 27 C3
Lasborough Rd MK10 . . . . . . 30 C3
Lascelles Ct MK15 . . . . 12 A1
Laser Cl MK5. . . . . 34 A4
Lastingham Gr MK4. . . . . 43 C4
Latimer MK11 . . . . 16 C2
Launceston Ct MK5 . . . . 33 C4
Launde **1** MK10. . . . . 30 B3
Laurel Ct MK8 . . . . 25 A1
Laurels The MK1. . . . . 46 B3
Lavender Gr MK7 . . . . 37 B3
Lawnsmead Gdns MK16. . . . . 3 C3
Lawrence Wlk MK16 . . . . 2 B3
Lawson Pl MK5 . . . . 33 C3
Leaberry MK13 . . . . 9 C2
Leadenhall Rdbt MK6. . . . . . 27 B1
Leafield Rise MK8 . . . . 25 A4
Learoyd Way LU7. . . . . 71 A4
Leary Cres MK16. . . . . 4 A2
Leasowe Pl MK13 . . . . 20 A1
Leck Ho **10** LU7. . . . . 66 A1
Ledburn Gr LU7 . . . . 69 B4
Ledbury MK14. . . . . 11 A3
Leedon Lower Sch LU7 . . . . . 70 C4
Lee Ho **2** MK2. . . . . 46 A2
Leigh Hill MK4 . . . . 44 B4
Leighton Buzzard Narrow
  Gauge Railway★ LU7 . . . . . 66 C3
Leighton Buzzard Sta LU7 . . 65 B1
Leighton Mid Sch LU7 . . . . . 69 C4
Leighton Rd
  Heath and Reach LU7. . . . . . 63 A2
  Leighton Buzzard LU7. . . . . . 65 C1
  Soulbury LU7 . . . . 64 B3
  Stoke Hammond MK17. . . . . 58 A1
  Wing LU7 . . . . 68 A1
Leisure Plaza★ MK9. . . . . 26 C2
Lenborough Cl MK18 . . . . . . 74 B3
Lenborough Ct MK15 . . . . . . 28 C4
Lenborough Rd MK18. . . . . . 74 B3
Lennon Dr MK8. . . . . 25 B1
Lennox Rd MK2. . . . . 46 B1
Lenthall Cl MK13 . . . . 19 B3
Leominster Gate **4** MK10. 30 A3
Leonardslee MK4 . . . . 43 A4
Leon Ave MK2 . . . . 46 B2
Leon Sch & Sports Coll
  MK2. . . . . 54 C3
Leopard Dr MK15. . . . . 11 C1
Leopold Rd LU7 . . . . 65 A1
Lester Ct MK7. . . . . 30 C1
Leven Cl
  Leighton Buzzard LU7. . . . . . 64 B1
  Milton Keynes MK2. . . . . 55 A3
Levens Hall Dr MK4 . . . . 43 A3
Lewes Ho MK3 . . . . 44 B1
Lewis Cl MK16. . . . . 2 B3
Leyland Pl **3** MK6 . . . . 27 B3
Leys Ct MK5. . . . . 26 B2
Leys Rd MK5 . . . . 26 B2
Leys The Buckingham MK18 . . 71 B3
  Woburn Sands MK17 . . . . . . 39 C2
Lichfield Down MK7. . . . . 37 C3
Liddell Way LU7 . . . . 71 A3
Lightfoot Ct MK7 . . . . 37 A3
Lilac Cl MK17. . . . . 52 C1
Lilleshall Ave MK10 . . . . 29 C3
Limbaud Cl MK7. . . . . 37 B3
Lime Ave MK18 . . . . 75 B3
Lime Cl MK16. . . . . 3 A1
Lime Gr Leighton Buzzard LU7 . 65 B2
  Woburn Sands MK17. . . . . . . 39 C2
Limerick La MK9. . . . . 21 C1
Limes The
  Milton Keynes,Fenny Stratford
    MK2. 46 C3
  Milton Keynes MK11. . . . . . . 16 C3
Lincesdale Gr MK5. . . . . 26 B3
Lincoln MK14. . . . . 10 B2
Lincolnshire Cl MK3 . . . . 44 C3

Lincombe Slade LU7 . . . . 65 B2
Linden Gr MK14 . . . . 11 A2
Lindisfarne Dr MK10 . . . . 30 A3
Lindler Ct LU7 . . . . 70 A4
Lindores Croft MK10 . . . . 30 B3
Linford Ave MK16 . . . . 2 C2
Linford Day Hospl MK12 . . . . 18 A3
Linford La
  Milton Keynes,Willen MK15 . . . 12 C1
  Milton Keynes,Woolstone
  MK15 . . . . 22 A1
Lingfield MK12 . . . . 18 C2
Linney Ct MK4 . . . . 43 B3
Linslade Lower Sch LU7 . . . . . 65 A1
Linslade Mid Sch LU7 . . . . 69 B3
Linslade Rd LU7 . . . . 62 B2
Lintlaw Pl MK3 . . . . 35 B1
Linton Cl MK13 . . . . 20 A2
Linwood Gr LU7 . . . . 70 B4
Linx The MK3 . . . . 45 B4
Lipscombe Dr MK18 . . . . 71 A1
Lipscomb La MK5 . . . . 26 A1
Lissel Rd MK6 . . . . 36 C3
Little Balmer MK18 . . . . 75 A2
Littlecote MK8 . . . . 26 A3
Little Dunmow MK10 . . . . 30 A3
Little Habton 3 MK4 . . . . 43 C4
Little Hame MK10 . . . . 23 A1
Little Linford La MK16,MK19 . . 2 A2
Little London MK19 . . . . 14 C2
Littlemere MK8 . . . . 25 A3
Little Stanton MK14 . . . . 10 C2
Little Stocking MK5 . . . . 33 B1
Livesey Hill MK15 . . . . 33 C3
Livingstone Dr MK15 . . . . 22 A3
Lloyds MK6 . . . . 28 A1
Lochy Dr LU7 . . . . 64 C1
Locke Rd MK2 . . . . 46 A2
Lock La MK19 . . . . 7 A4
Lockton Ct MK4 . . . . 33 C1
Lockview Cotts MK1 . . . . 46 C3
Lock View La MK1 . . . . 46 C3
Lodge Gate MK14 . . . . 11 A1
Lodge La MK17 . . . . 58 A1
Lodge Park The MK16 . . . . 3 B2
Logan Rock MK4 . . . . 43 C2
Lomond Dr
  Leighton Buzzard LU7 . . . . 64 C1
  Milton Keynes MK2 . . . . 55 A2
London End La MK17 . . . . 48 B3
London End MK17 . . . . 53 A2
London Ho MK11 . . . . 16 B3
London Rd
  Buckingham MK18 . . . . 75 A2
  Loughton MK5 . . . . 26 B1
  Milton Keynes MK16 . . . . 23 C3
  Milton Keynes,Stony Stratford
  MK11 . . . . 16 C3
  Newport Pagnell MK16 . . . . 4 B1
  Old Stratford MK19 . . . . 6 B1
Long Ayres MK7 . . . . 37 B1
Longcross MK15 . . . . 21 B4
Longfellow Dr MK16 . . . . 2 C2
Longhedge MK7 . . . . 47 B4
Longleat Ct 7 MK8 . . . . 25 C3
Long Meadow Sch MK5 . . . . . . 33 A1
Longpeak Cl MK4 . . . . 43 C3
Longville MK12 . . . . 8 A1
Lord Grey Sch MK3 . . . . 45 A3
Lords Cl MK2 . . . . 46 A3
Loriner Pl MK14 . . . . 21 B4
Loseley Ct MK8 . . . . 25 C3
Lothersdale MK13 . . . . 19 C3
Lothian Cl MK3 . . . . 44 C4
Loughton Manor First Sch
  MK5 . . . . 26 A2
Loughton Middle Sch MK5 . . 26 A1
Loughton Rdbt MK8 . . . . 25 C2
Loughton Rd MK13 . . . . 19 B1
Lovat Mid Sch MK16 . . . . 3 C1
Lovat St MK16 . . . . 3 C2
Lovatt Dr MK3 . . . . 44 C2
Lovent Dr LU7 . . . . 66 B1
Lower Eighth St MK9 . . . . 27 B4

Lower End MK17 . . . . 52 C1
Lower Fourth St MK9 . . . . 27 A3
Lower Ninth St MK9 . . . . 27 B4
Lower Second St MK9 . . . . 27 A3
Lower Stonehayes MK14 . . . . . 11 B1
Lower Tenth St MK9 . . . . 27 C4
Lower Third St MK9 . . . . 27 A3
Lower Twelfth St MK9 . . . . 21 A1
Lower Way MK17 . . . . 59 B3
Lower Wharf MK18 . . . . 71 A1
Lowick Pl 4 MK4 . . . . 43 C4
Lowland Rd MK13 . . . . 44 A2
Lowndes Gr MK5 . . . . 25 C1
Loxbeare Dr MK4 . . . . 34 A2
Loyne Cl LU7 . . . . 64 C2
Lucas Pl MK6 . . . . 29 A2
Luccombe MK4 . . . . 34 B1
Lucy La MK5 . . . . 26 B2
Ludgate MK6 . . . . 27 B1
Ludlow Cl MK3 . . . . 45 A1
Lufford Pk MK14 . . . . 11 B2
Luke Pl MK10 . . . . 23 A1
Lullingstone Dr MK13 . . . . 19 A3
Lundholme MK13 . . . . 19 C3
Luttlemarsh MK7 . . . . 37 B3
Lutyens Gr MK7 . . . . 38 B3
Luxborough Gr MK4 . . . . 34 A2
Lydiard MK8 . . . . 25 B3
Lynmouth Cres MK4 . . . . 34 B2
Lynott Cl MK8 . . . . 32 C4
Lyon Rd MK1 . . . . 45 C4
Lyra Gdns LU7 . . . . 67 A2
Lywood Rd LU7 . . . . 70 C4

M

McConnell Dr MK12 . . . . 18 C4
McKenzie Cl MK18 . . . . 74 C4
Maconi Croft MK5 . . . . 34 A3
Magdalen Cl MK11 . . . . 16 B4
Magdalen Ho MK11 . . . . 16 B4
Magenta Cl MK2 . . . . 55 A4
Magpie Cl MK5 . . . . 33 C2
Mahler Cl MK7 . . . . 38 A3
Maidenhead Ave MK13 . . . . . . 20 A1
Maids Moreton CE Sch
  MK18 . . . . 71 A3
Maidstone Rd MK10 . . . . 30 A4
Main St Buckingham MK18 . . . 71 B3
  Chackmore MK18 . . . . 72 A4
  Cosgrove MK19 . . . . 7 A4
Malbons Ct MK6 . . . . 27 B1
Malins Gate MK14 . . . . 11 A2
Mallard Dr MK18 . . . . 75 A4
Malletts Cl MK11 . . . . 16 C3
Mallow Gate MK14 . . . . 20 C2
Maltings The
  Chackmore MK18 . . . . 72 A4
  Leighton Buzzard LU7 . . . . 70 B4
Malton Cl MK10 . . . . 29 C3
Malvern Dr
  Leighton Buzzard LU7 . . . . 64 C2
  Milton Keynes MK11 . . . . 17 B2
Mandeville Cl MK10 . . . . 30 C4
Manifold La MK4,MK5 . . . . 33 C1
Mannock Way LU7 . . . . 71 A3
Manor Cl Cosgrove MK19 . . . . . 7 A4
  Milton Keynes MK10 . . . . 23 A1
  Stoke Hammond MK17 . . . . 58 A1
Manor Cotts MK12 . . . . 8 A1
Manor Ct LU7 . . . . 65 B4
Manor Dr MK19 . . . . 9 A4
Manorfields Rd MK19 . . . . 15 C4
Manor Gdns MK18 . . . . 71 A2
Manor Pk MK18 . . . . 71 B4
Manor Rd
  Milton Keynes,Bletchley
  MK2 . . . . 46 C2
  Milton Keynes,Wolverton
  MK12 . . . . 8 A1
  Newport Pagnell MK16 . . . . 2 C2
  Newton Longville MK17 . . . . . . 53 A1
Manor St MK18 . . . . 74 B4
Manse Cl MK11 . . . . 16 B4
Mansel Cl MK19 . . . . 7 A4

Mansell Cl MK5 . . . . 33 B4
Manshead Ct MK11 . . . . 17 A3
Mapledean MK12 . . . . 18 C2
Mapledurham MK7 . . . . 37 C1
Maple Gr Milton Keynes MK2 . . 46 C2
  Woburn Sands MK17 . . . . 39 C2
Mapperton Cl MK4 . . . . 43 A3
Mara Pl MK9 . . . . 21 B1
March Edge MK18 . . . . 71 A1
March Mdw MK7 . . . . 31 A1
Mardle Rd LU7 . . . . 69 B4
Maree Cl
  Leighton Buzzard LU7 . . . . 64 C1
  Milton Keynes MK2 . . . . 54 C3
Mare Leys MK18 . . . . 75 B4
Margam Cres MK10 . . . . 30 A3
Margaret Powell Sq MK9 . . . 21 A1
Marigold Pl MK14 . . . . 20 C2
Marina Cl MK12 . . . . 18 B4
Marina Rdbt MK6 . . . . 28 C1
Marjoram Pl MK14 . . . . 20 C2
Markenfield Pl MK4 . . . . 42 C3
Market Hill
  Buckingham MK18 . . . . 72 C1
  Milton Keynes MK6 . . . . 28 B2
Market Mews 8 LU7 . . . . 66 A1
Market Pl MK17 . . . . 51 A1
Market Sq Buckingham MK18 . . 72 C1
  Leighton Buzzard LU7 . . . . 66 A1
  Milton Keynes MK11 . . . . 16 B3
Markhams Cl MK18 . . . . 74 C4
Marlborough Gate MK9 . . . . . 21 A1
Marlborough St
  Milton Keynes,Neath Hill
  MK14 . . . . 20 C4
  Milton Keynes,Tinkers Bridge
  MK6 . . . . 36 B4
Marley Fields LU7 . . . . 71 A4
Marley Gr MK8 . . . . 25 B1
Marlow Dr MK16 . . . . 2 C2
Marquis Cl MK17 . . . . 51 A1
Marram Ct MK6 . . . . 35 B3
Marron La MK12 . . . . 18 A3
Marshall Court Ind Pk MK1 . 45 C3
Marshalls La MK15 . . . . 28 C4
Marshaw Pl 3 MK4 . . . . 44 A4
Marsh Dr MK14 . . . . 11 A3
Marsh End Rd MK16 . . . . 3 C1
Marshworth MK6 . . . . 36 B4
Martell Cl MK7 . . . . 37 B1
Martin Cl Buckingham MK18 . . 75 B3
  Milton Keynes MK14 . . . . 20 C4
Martingale Pl MK14 . . . . 21 A3
Martins Dr The LU7 . . . . 65 C2
Marwood Cl MK4 . . . . 34 B1
Maryland Rd MK15 . . . . 12 A2
Mary MacManus Dr MK18 . . 72 C1
Masefield Cl MK16 . . . . 2 C2
Masefield Gr MK3 . . . . 45 B1
Maslin Dr MK6 . . . . 35 C3
Mason MK14 . . . . 10 B2
Massie Cl MK15 . . . . 21 C4
Mathiesen Rd MK13 . . . . 1C A3
Matilda Gdns MK5 . . . . 33 C3
Matthew Ct MK5 . . . . 33 C4
Maudsley Cl MK5 . . . . 34 A4
Maulden Gdns MK14 . . . . 11 C2
Mavoncliff Dr MK4 . . . . 43 B2
Maxham MK5 . . . . 33 B1
Maybach Ct MK5 . . . . 33 C3
Mayditch Pl MK13 . . . . 20 A1
Mayer Gdns MK5 . . . . 34 A3
Maynard Cl MK13 . . . . 19 B1
Meadfarling Mid Sch MK6 . . 27 C1
Meadow Gdns MK18 . . . . 75 A2
Meadow La MK10 . . . . 23 B1
Meadow Row MK18 . . . . 72 C1
Meadows The MK19 . . . . 15 C4
Meadowsweet MK7 . . . . 37 C3
Meadow View MK17 . . . . 40 B4
Meadow Way LU7 . . . . 67 A1
Meadow Wlk MK18 . . . . 72 C1
Meads Cl MK13 . . . . 10 A2
Mead The LU7 . . . . 60 A1
Meadway Buckingham MK18 . . 74 C2

Meadway continued
  Leighton Buzzard LU7 . . . . 66 C2
Meadway The MK5 . . . . 26 A1
Medale Rd MK6 . . . . 35 C3
Medbourne Rdbt MK8 . . . . . . 32 C4
Medeswell MK4 . . . . 34 C1
Medhurst MK8 . . . . 25 B4
Medland MK6 . . . . 29 A1
Medway Cl MK16 . . . . 4 A1
Melbourne Terr MK13 . . . . 9 C1
Melfort Dr
  Leighton Buzzard LU7 . . . . 68 B4
  Milton Keynes MK2 . . . . 55 A2
Melick Rd MK6 . . . . 35 C2
Mellish Ct MK3 . . . . 45 B4
Melrose Ave MK3 . . . . 35 B1
Melton MK14 . . . . 10 B2
Mendelssohn Gr MK7 . . . . 38 A2
Menteith Cl MK2 . . . . 54 C3
Mentmore Ct 2 MK8 . . . . 25 C2
Mentmore Gdns LU7 . . . . 69 B3
Mentmore Rd LU7 . . . . 69 B3
Mentone Ave MK17 . . . . 40 B2
Menzies Ct MK5 . . . . 33 C2
Mercers Dr MK13 . . . . 19 C4
Merchant Pl MK10 . . . . 22 C1
Mercury Gr MK8 . . . . 25 B1
Mercury Way LU7 . . . . 67 A2
Merebrook First Sch MK4 . . 34 A1
Meriland Ct MK2 . . . . 55 B2
Merlewood Dr MK5 . . . . 33 A2
Merlins Ct LU7 . . . . 66 A1
Merlin Wlk MK6 . . . . 28 B2
Mersey Cl MK3 . . . . 44 C3
Mersey Way MK3 . . . . 44 C3
Merthen Gr MK4 . . . . 43 C2
Merton Dr MK6 . . . . 35 B2
Metcalfe Gr MK14 . . . . 12 A4
Michigan Dr
  Milton Keynes MK15 . . . . 12 B2
  Newport Pagnell MK15 . . . . . . 12 B3
Mickleton MK15 . . . . 21 B4
Middlefield Cl MK18 . . . . 71 B1
Middle Gn LU7 . . . . 66 C2
Middlesex Dr MK3 . . . . 45 A3
Middle Slade MK18 . . . . 74 C2
Middleton MK14 . . . . 11 A1
Middleton Prim Sch MK10 . . 22 C1
Middleton Way LU7 . . . . 71 A3
Midsummer Arc MK9 . . . . 20 C1
Midsummer Bvd MK9 . . . . 27 B4
Midsummer Pl MK9 . . . . 27 B4
Midsummer Rdbt MK9 . . . . . . 26 C3
Midway LU7 . . . . 66 C1
Mikern Cl MK2 . . . . 46 A2
Milburn Ave MK6 . . . . 27 B2
Milebush LU7 . . . . 64 C2
Milecastle MK13 . . . . 19 B3
Miles Ave LU7 . . . . 66 B1
Miles Cl MK14 . . . . 2 C1
Milesmere MK8 . . . . 25 A3
Miletree Ct LU7 . . . . 66 B2
Milfoil Ave MK14 . . . . 20 C2
Milford Ave MK11 . . . . 16 C2
Millbank LU7 . . . . 65 C2
Millbank Pl MK7 . . . . 30 B2
Mill Ct MK12 . . . . 17 B3
Millers Cl LU7 . . . . 67 A1
Millers Way MK12 . . . . 18 B3
Millhayes MK14 . . . . 11 B2
Mill Ho MK18 . . . . 74 B4
Millholm Rise MK6 . . . . 36 C3
Millington Gate MK15 . . . . . . 12 C1
Mill La Aspley Guise MK17 . . . 40 A3
  Buckingham MK18 . . . . 74 B4
  Great Brickhill MK17 . . . . 58 B4
  Milton Keynes,Bradville MK13 . . 9 C1
  Milton Keynes,Stony Stratford
  MK11 . . . . 16 A3
  Milton Keynes,Woolstone
  MK15 . . . . 22 A1

Mill Rd
2 Leighton Buzzard LU7 . . . .**65** C2
Leighton Buzzard LU7. . . . .**66** A2
Milton Keynes MK2. . . . .**46** C1
Mill Sq MK12 . . . .**17** B3
Mill St MK16. . . . .**3** C3
Millstream Way LU7 . . . .**65** C1
Mill Terr MK12 . . . .**17** B4
Mill The MK12 . . . .**7** A1
Mill Way MK17. . . . .**40** B3
Milton Dr MK16. . . . .**4** A2
Milton Gr MK3. . . . .**45** A1
Milton Keynes Central Sta
MK9. . . . .**26** C3
Milton Keynes Coll (Bletchley
Ctr) MK3 . . . .**45** C2
Milton Keynes Coll MK6 . . . .**27** C1
Milton Keynes Coll
(Wolverton Ctr) MK12. . . . . .**17** C4
Milton Keynes General Hospl
MK6. . . . .**28** B1
Milton Keynes Materials
Recycling Factory★ MK12 . . **8** B2
Milton Keynes Mus★ MK12 . **18** B3
Milton Keynes Prep Sch
MK3. . . . .**44** B2
Milton Rd
Milton Keynes,Broughton
MK10. . . . .**23** C1
Milton Keynes,Willen MK15 . . . .**12** C1
Walton MK7 . . . .**37** A4
Minerva Gdns MK7 . . . .**30** C1
Minorca Gr MK5. . . . .**33** B2
Minshull Cl MK18 . . . .**72** C1
Minstrel Ct MK13 . . . .**10** A1
Minton Cl MK14 . . . .**11** C3
Mitcham Pl MK13. . . . .**20** B1
Mithras Gdns MK7 . . . .**38** A4
Mitre Ct MK18 . . . .**74** B3
Mitre St MK18 . . . .**74** B3
Moat House The MK18 . . . .**74** C4
Moeran Cl MK7. . . . .**38** A3
Monellan Cres MK7. . . . .**37** B1
Monellan Gr MK7. . . . .**47** B4
Monkston Comb Sch MK10 . .**30** B3
Monkston Rdbt MK10 . . . .**30** B4
Monks Way MK12,MK13,MK14,
MK15. . . . .**20** A4
Monmouth Gr MK4 . . . .**42** C3
Monro Ave MK8 . . . .**25** B1
Montagu Dr MK6 . . . .**28** B2
Montgomery Cl LU7 . . . .**66** B3
Montgomery Cres MK15 . . . . .**12** A1
Moon St MK12. . . . .**18** B4
Moorfield MK17 . . . .**53** A1
Moorfoot MK11. . . . .**17** B2
Moorgate MK6 . . . .**27** C1
Moorhen Way MK18 . . . .**75** A4
Moorhouse Path LU7 . . . .**71** A3
Moorhouse Way LU7 . . . .**71** A3
Moorings The MK18. . . . .**74** B4
Moorland Fst Sch MK6 . . . . . .**35** C3
Moor Pk MK3. . . . .**44** B2
Moors Cl MK19 . . . .**14** C3
Morar Cl LU7. . . . .**64** C1
Moray Pl MK3 . . . .**45** A4
Mordaunts Ct MK15. . . . .**28** C4
Morebath Gr MK4. . . . .**34** A2
Moreton Dr MK18. . . . .**71** A2
Moreton Rd MK18 . . . .**72** C2
Morland Dr MK8. . . . .**32** B4
Morley Cres MK7 . . . .**38** B2
Morrell Cl MK5 . . . .**33** C3
Morrison Ct MK8 . . . .**32** C4
Morris Wlk MK16 . . . .**2** C2
Mortain Cl MK7. . . . .**37** C1
Mortons Fork MK13. . . . .**19** A4
Mossdale MK13 . . . .**19** C3
Mount Ave MK1. . . . .**36** C1
Mountbatten Gdns LU7 . . . . . .**66** B3
Mount Farm Ind Est MK1 . . .**36** B2
Mount Farm Rdbt MK1. . . . . . .**36** B2

Mounthill Ave MK19 . . . .**6** A1
Mount Pleasant MK17. . . . . . .**41** A2
Mount Pleasant Cl MK18 . . . .**74** B3
Mount Pleasant
Milton Keynes MK6. . . . .**36** C3
Soulbury LU7 . . . .**60** A1
Stoke Hammond MK17. . . . .**58** A1
Mountsfield Cl MK16. . . . .**3** B1
Mount The
Aspley Guise MK17. . . . .**40** B2
Milton Keynes MK6. . . . .**36** C2
Mowbray Dr LU7 . . . .**65** A1
Mozart Cl MK7 . . . .**38** A2
Muddiford La MK4. . . . .**34** B2
Muirfield Dr MK3. . . . .**44** B3
Mullen Ave MK14 . . . .**21** A2
Mullion Pl MK6 . . . .**28** A3
Murrey Cl MK5 . . . .**34** A3
Mursley Ct MK11 . . . .**17** A3
Musgrove Pl MK5. . . . .**33** A4
Myrtle Bank MK12 . . . .**18** C3

N

Nairn Ct MK3 . . . .**44** C4
Naisby Dr MK17 . . . .**59** B3
Naphill Pl MK13 . . . .**20** A1
Napier St MK2. . . . .**46** B2
Narrow Path MK17. . . . .**39** C1
Naseby Cl MK16 . . . .**2** C1
Naseby Ct Buckingham MK18 . . .**71** A2
Milton Keynes MK13. . . . .**19** C4
Nash Croft MK4. . . . .**43** C2
Nathanial Cl MK5. . . . .**33** C3
National Badminton Ctr
MK8. . . . .**26** A3
National Bowl The★ MK6 . . .**34** C3
National Hockey Stadium
MK9. . . . .**26** C3
Neapland MK6. . . . .**35** C3
Neath Cres MK3 . . . .**45** B4
Neath Hill Rdbt MK15 . . . .**21** B4
Nebular Ct LU7 . . . .**66** C2
Neilson Ct MK7 . . . .**38** A3
Nelson Cl MK8. . . . .**32** C4
Nelson Ct MK18 . . . .**74** B4
Nelson Rd LU7 . . . .**66** B3
Nelson St MK18. . . . .**74** B4
Nene Cl MK16 . . . .**3** C1
Nene Dr MK3 . . . .**44** C2
Neptune Gdns LU7. . . . .**67** A2
Ness Way MK2. . . . .**55** A3
Netherfield Rdbt MK6. . . . .**28** C1
Nether Gr MK5 . . . .**33** C1
Netley Ct MK10 . . . .**30** A3
Nettlecombe MK4 . . . .**34** A1
Nettleton Cl LU7. . . . .**70** C4
Nevis Cl LU7. . . . .**64** C1
Nevis Gr MK2. . . . .**55** B2
Newark Ct MK7. . . . .**37** B1
Newbolt Cl MK16 . . . .**2** B3
New Bradwell Comb Sch
MK13. . . . .**9** B1
Newbridge Oval MK4 . . . .**33** C1
Newbury Ct MK3. . . . .**53** A4
Newby Pl MK4. . . . .**43** C4
New Chapter Comb sch
MK6. . . . .**35** B3
New College Ct MK18 . . . .**72** A4
Newlyn Pl MK6 . . . .**28** A4
Newmans Cl MK14 . . . .**11** A3
Newman Way LU7 . . . .**66** B1
Newmarket Ct MK10 . . . .**30** C4
Newport Rd
Milton Keynes MK10. . . . .**31** A3
Milton Keynes,New Bradwell
MK13. . . . .**9** C2
Milton Keynes,Oakgrove
MK15. . . . .**28** C4
Milton Keynes,Willen MK15 . . . .**12** C1
Milton Keynes,Woughton on t G
MK6. . . . .**29** A3
Wavendon MK17 . . . .**31** B1
Woburn MK17. . . . .**51** A2
Woughton On T G MK6 . . . .**29** A2

Newport Rd *continued*
Woughton Park MK6. . . . .**36** B4
Newquay Cl MK4 . . . .**43** A3
New Rd LU7 . . . .**65** B1
New St MK11 . . . .**16** B3
Newton Longville CE Comb
Sch MK17 . . . .**53** A1
Newton Rd MK3 . . . .**53** B4
Newton Way LU7 . . . .**71** A4
Nicholas Mead MK14 . . . .**11** B2
Nicholson Dr LU7. . . . .**71** A3
Nicholson Gr MK8 . . . .**32** C4
Nielson Ct MK7 . . . .**38** B3
Nightingale Cres MK13. . . . .**9** C1
Nightingale Pl MK18 . . . .**71** A1
Nixons Cl MK6. . . . .**34** C4
Noble Cl MK15. . . . .**11** C1
Noon Layer Dr MK10 . . . .**22** C1
Norbrek MK8 . . . .**25** B4
Norfolk Ho 6 MK3. . . . .**45** A3
Norman Cres MK10 . . . .**22** C1
Normandy Way MK3 . . . .**44** C4
Norrington MK8 . . . .**25** B4
Northampton Rd
Cosgrove MK19 . . . .**6** B2
Cosgrove MK19 . . . .**6** B3
Lathbury MK16 . . . .**3** C4
Northcourt LU7. . . . .**66** A3
Northcroft MK5. . . . .**34** A4
North Ct MK10. . . . .**30** B3
North Eighth St MK9. . . . .**20** C1
North Elder Rdbt MK9 . . . .**26** C3
North Eleventh St MK9. . . . . . .**20** C1
Northend Ct MK18 . . . .**72** C1
Northend Sq MK18. . . . .**72** C1
Northfield Dr MK15 . . . .**23** A3
Northfield Rdbt MK10. . . . .**23** B3
North Fifth St MK9. . . . .**27** A4
North Fourteenth St MK9 . . .**21** A2
North Fourth St MK9. . . . .**27** A4
North Gate MK2 . . . .**46** A3
North Grafton Rdbt MK13 . . . .**26** C4
North La MK7 . . . .**29** B1
Northleigh MK4 . . . .**44** B4
North Ninth St MK9. . . . .**20** C1
North Overgate Rdbt MK15. .**21** C3
North Ridge MK6 . . . .**28** B3
North Row
Milton Keynes MK9. . . . .**20** C1
Milton Keynes MK9. . . . .**26** C4
North Saxon Rdbt MK14. . . . . .**20** B1
North Secklow Rdbt MK14 . . .**20** C1
North Second St MK9 . . . .**26** C4
North Seventh St MK9 . . . .**27** A4
North Sixth St MK9 . . . .**27** A4
North Skeldon Rdbt MK9. . . . .**21** B2
North Sq MK16 . . . .**3** C3
North Star Dr LU7 . . . .**66** C2
North St
Leighton Buzzard LU7. . . . .**66** A1
Milton Keynes,Bradville MK13 . . .**9** C1
Milton Keynes,Fenny Stratford
MK2. . . . .**46** A3
North Tenth St MK9 . . . .**20** C1
North Third St MK9 . . . .**26** C4
North Thirteenth St MK9 . . . .**21** A1
North Twelfth St MK9 . . . .**21** A1
North Way
Deanshanger NN12 . . . .**14** C3
Potterspury NN12. . . . .**5** A4
Northwich MK6. . . . .**29** A1
North Witan Rdbt MK13 . . . . . .**27** A4
Norton Leys MK7 . . . .**30** C1
Norton's Pl MK18. . . . .**74** B4
Nortons The MK7. . . . .**37** C1
Norwood La MK16 . . . .**3** B1
Nottingham Gr MK3 . . . .**44** C4
Nova Lodge MK4 . . . .**43** C4
Novello Croft MK7 . . . .**38** B2
Nuneham Gr MK4. . . . .**33** A1
Nursery Gdns MK13. . . . .**19** B2
Nutmeg Cl MK7. . . . .**37** C3

O

Oak Bank Dr LU7 . . . .**62** C1
Oak Bank Sch LU7. . . . .**62** C1
Oak Ct MK9 . . . .**27** B4
Oaken Head MK4 . . . .**44** A4
Oakgrove Rdbt MK10 . . . .**29** C4
Oakham Rise MK4 . . . .**42** C3
Oakhill Cl MK5 . . . .**32** C4
Oakhill Rdbt MK5 . . . .**32** B3
Oakhill Rd
Milton Keynes,Hazeley MK5. . . . .**32** B3
Milton Keynes,Shenley Church End
MK5. . . . .**33** A4
Oakley Gdns MK15. . . . .**21** C3
Oakley Gn LU7 . . . .**66** B3
Oakridge MK4 . . . .**34** C2
Oakridge Pk LU7 . . . .**70** B3
Oaks The LU7. . . . .**62** C3
Oaktree Ct MK15. . . . .**12** B1
Oakwood Dr MK2 . . . .**46** C1
Oatfield Gdns LU7 . . . .**67** A1
Octavian Dr MK13 . . . .**19** A3
Odell Cl MK6 . . . .**28** C2
Oldbrook Bvd MK6. . . . .**27** B2
Oldbrook Fst Sch MK6. . . . .**27** B2
Oldcastle Croft MK4 . . . .**43** B3
Old Chapel Mews LU7 . . . .**70** A4
Olde Bell Cl MK17 . . . .**58** A1
Olde Bell La MK5 . . . .**26** A1
Old Gaol Mus★ MK18. . . . . . .**72** C1
Old Groveway MK6 . . . .**36** B3
Old Linslade Rd LU7 . . . .**62** A1
Old Maltings The MK18. . . . . .**74** B3
Old Rd LU7 . . . .**65** B1
Old School Ct
2 Leighton Buzzard LU7. . . . . . .**66** A1
Buckingham MK18 . . . .**74** B4
Old School La MK17 . . . .**58** A2
Old Stable Yd MK19 . . . .**6** B1
Old Stratford Prim Sch
MK19. . . . .**15** C4
Old Wolverton Rd MK12. . . . . . .**8** B2
Oliver Rd MK2 . . . .**46** A2
Omega Ct LU7. . . . .**66** C2
O'Neill Rd MK8 . . . .**32** B4
Onslow Ct MK7 . . . .**37** B2
Opal Dr MK15 . . . .**23** A2
Open University (Walton Hall)
The MK7 . . . .**29** C1
Orbison Ct MK8. . . . .**25** A1
Orchard Cl
Milton Keynes MK3. . . . .**45** A1
Newton Longville MK17 . . . .**52** C1
Orchard Dene MK18 . . . .**72** C1
Orchard Dr LU7. . . . .**69** A4
Orchard Ho MK12. . . . .**18** B4
Orford Ct MK5 . . . .**33** C4
Oriel Cl MK12. . . . .**17** C4
Orion Way LU7 . . . .**67** A2
Orkney Cl MK3 . . . .**45** A4
Ormonde MK14 . . . .**10** C1
Ormsgill Ct MK13 . . . .**19** C3
Orne Gdns MK15. . . . .**11** C1
Orpington Gr MK5 . . . .**33** C2
Ortensia Dr MK7. . . . .**30** C1
Orwell Cl MK16 . . . .**2** B3
Osborne St MK2 . . . .**46** A1
Osbourne St MK12. . . . .**18** B4
Osier La MK5. . . . .**33** C2
Osier Way MK18 . . . .**74** B2
Osprey Cl MK6. . . . .**28** B2
Osprey Wlk MK18. . . . .**75** B3
Osterley Cl MK16 . . . .**3** B1
Ostlers La MK11 . . . .**16** B4
Otterburn Cres MK5 . . . .**32** B3
Otter Cl MK2 . . . .**44** B3
Otters Brook MK18 . . . .**75** A3
Ousebank St MK16. . . . .**3** C3
Ousebank Way MK11. . . . .**16** B3
Ousedale Sch MK16 . . . .**3** A1
Ouzel Cl MK3 . . . .**44** C3
Oval The MK6. . . . .**27** B1
Overend Cl MK13 . . . .**19** B2
Overend Green La LU7 . . . .**63** B4

Overgate MK6,MK9,MK14 . . . . . **21** C2
Overn Ave MK18 . . . . **72** B1
Overn Cl MK18 . . . . **72** C1
Overn Cres MK18 . . . . **72** B1
Oversley Ct MK14 . . . . **11** C3
Overstreet MK15 . . . . **21** B4
Oville Cl MK5 . . . . **33** C3
Oxendon Ct LU7 . . . . **65** C4
Oxfield Park Dr MK19 . . . . **6** B1
Oxford St
  Milton Keynes,Fenny Stratford
  MK2 . . . . **46** A2
  Milton Keynes,Stony Stratford
  MK11 . . . . **16** B3
  Milton Keynes,Wolverton
  MK12 . . . . **18** B4
Oxhouse Ct MK5 . . . . **33** B1
Oxley Park Rdbt MK5 . . . . **33** A1
Oxman La MK12 . . . . **17** B3
Oxwich Gr MK4 . . . . **43** C2

P

Paddock Cl MK14 . . . . **11** A2
Paddocks The LU7 . . . . **65** C2
Paddock The MK18 . . . . **71** A4
Paddock Way MK2 . . . . **46** B3
Padstow Ave MK6 . . . . **27** C3
Page Hill Ave MK18 . . . . **71** A1
Page's Almshouses **5** LU7 . . **66** A2
Page's Ind Pk LU7 . . . . **70** B3
Pagg's Ct MK16 . . . . **3** C2
Pagoda Rdbt MK15 . . . . **22** A3
Palace Sq MK6 . . . . **27** C1
Pannier Pl MK14 . . . . **21** B3
Paprika Ct MK7 . . . . **37** C3
Paradise MK17 . . . . **53** A2
Park Ave MK16 . . . . **3** A2
Park Cl MK19 . . . . **7** B4
Parker Cl MK13 . . . . **19** B4
Park Gdns MK3 . . . . **45** B3
Park House Dr MK5 . . . . **33** A4
Parklands MK14 . . . . **10** C3
Park Mews LU7 . . . . **70** A4
Parkminster MK10 . . . . **30** A3
Park Rd MK11 . . . . **16** B3
Parkside MK4 . . . . **34** C1
Park St Woburn MK17 . . . . **51** A1
  Woburn MK17 . . . . **51** B1
Park View Ct **4** LU7 . . . . . . **65** B1
Park View MK16 . . . . **3** C2
Parkway Bow Brickhill MK17 . . **48** B4
  Woburn Sands MK17 . . . . **39** B4
Parneleys MK10 . . . . **29** C4
Parrock La MK10 . . . . **30** A4
Parsley Cl MK7 . . . . **37** C3
Parsons Cres MK5 . . . . **34** A3
Partridge Cl MK18 . . . . **75** B3
Pascal Dr MK5 . . . . **32** C3
Passalewe La MK7 . . . . **31** A1
Passmore MK6 . . . . **36** B4
Pastern Pl MK14 . . . . **21** B3
Pateman Cl MK18 . . . . **72** B1
Patricks La MK19 . . . . **15** A2
Patriot Dr MK13 . . . . **26** B4
Pattison La MK15 . . . . **22** A1
Paxton Cres MK5 . . . . **33** C3
Paynes Ct MK18 . . . . **72** C1
Paynes Dr MK5 . . . . **26** A2
Peacock Hay MK4 . . . . **44** A4
Peacock Mews **6** LU7 . . . . . **66** A1
Pearse Gr MK7 . . . . **37** B2
Pear Tree La LU7 . . . . **66** A2
Peckover Ct **8** MK8 . . . . **25** C3
Peebles Pl MK3 . . . . **35** A1
Peel Rd MK12 . . . . **18** A4
Peers Dr MK17 . . . . **40** C1
Peers La MK5 . . . . **33** C4
Pegasus Rd LU7 . . . . **67** A2
Pelham Pl MK14 . . . . **21** A3
Pelton Ct MK5 . . . . **34** A3
Pembridge Gr MK4 . . . . **42** C3
Pembroke Ho **2** MK3 . . . . . . **45** A3
Pencarrow Pl MK6 . . . . **28** A3
Pendennis Ct MK4 . . . . **43** B2

Pengelly Ct MK6 . . . . **28** A3
Penhale Cl MK4 . . . . **43** C2
Penhow Rise MK4 . . . . **42** C3
Penina MK3 . . . . **44** B3
Penlee Rise MK4 . . . . **43** C2
Penley Way LU7 . . . . **70** A3
Penmon Ct MK10 . . . . **29** C3
Pennivale Cl LU7 . . . . **66** A2
Penn Rd MK2 . . . . **46** C2
Pennycress Way MK16 . . . . **2** B2
Pennycuik MK17 . . . . **59** B3
Pennyroyal MK7 . . . . **30** B1
Penryn Ave MK6 . . . . **28** A4
Pentewan Gate MK6 . . . . **27** C4
Pentlands MK11 . . . . **17** A2
Penwith Fst Sch MK6 . . . . **27** C3
Pepper Hill Fst Sch MK13 . . . . **9** C1
Percheron Cl MK14 . . . . **21** A3
Peregrine Cl MK6 . . . . **28** B2
Perivale MK10 . . . . **29** B3
Permayne MK13 . . . . **9** C1
Perracombe MK4 . . . . **34** C1
Perran Ave MK6 . . . . **28** A3
Pershore Croft **1** MK10 . . . . **30** A3
Perth Cl MK3 . . . . **45** A4
Peterborough Gate MK15 . . . . **22** A4
Petersham Cl MK16 . . . . **12** B4
Pettingrew Cl MK7 . . . . **37** C4
Petworth Ho **2** MK8 . . . . . . **25** C3
Petworth MK8 . . . . **25** B3
Pevensey Cl MK3 . . . . **44** C1
Peverel Dr MK1 . . . . **35** C1
Phillimore Cl MK15 . . . . **12** A1
Phillip Ct MK5 . . . . **33** C4
Phoebe La MK17 . . . . **38** C4
Phoebe's Orch MK17 . . . . **58** A1
Phoenix Cl LU7 . . . . **67** A2
Phoenix Dr MK6 . . . . **34** C4
Pickering Dr MK4 . . . . **43** C4
Picton St MK4 . . . . **42** C3
Pightle Cres MK18 . . . . **72** C2
Pightle The
  Buckingham MK18 . . . . **72** C1
  Maids Moreton MK18 . . . . . . **71** B4
Pigott Dr MK5 . . . . **33** B3
Pilgrim St MK15 . . . . **21** B2
Pimpernel Gr MK7 . . . . **37** C4
Pinders Croft MK12 . . . . **17** C3
Pine Cl LU7 . . . . **66** A4
Pine Crest Mews LU7 . . . . **69** B4
Pine Gr MK17 . . . . **39** B2
Pineham Rdbt MK15 . . . . **22** C3
Pinewood Dr MK2 . . . . **46** C1
Pinfold MK7 . . . . **37** C4
Pinkard Ct MK6 . . . . **28** C2
Pinkle Hill Rd LU7 . . . . **62** C3
Pinks Cl MK5 . . . . **26** C2
Pinkworthy MK4 . . . . **34** B2
Pipard MK14 . . . . **11** A1
Pippin Cl MK16 . . . . **3** A1
Pipston Gn MK7 . . . . **30** B1
Pitcher La MK5 . . . . **26** B2
Pitchford Ave MK18 . . . . **71** A4
Pitchford Wlk MK18 . . . . **71** B1
Pitfield MK11 . . . . **17** C1
Pitt Gn MK18 . . . . **71** B1
Plantain Ct MK7 . . . . **37** C4
Plantation Pl MK5 . . . . **33** B2
Plantation Rd LU7 . . . . **62** B1
Pleshey Cl MK5 . . . . **33** C4
Plover Cl Buckingham MK18 . . **75** A3
  Newport Pagnell MK16 . . . . . . **3** A1
Plowman Cl MK12 . . . . **17** C3
Plumstead Ave MK13 . . . . **20** B1
Plum Tree La LU7 . . . . **66** A2
Plymouth Gr MK4 . . . . **43** C3
Pollys Yd MK14 . . . . **3** A3
Polmartin Ct MK6 . . . . **28** A3
Polruan Pl Fishermead MK6 . . **28** A3
  Milton Keynes MK6 . . . . **28** A3
Pomander Cres MK7 . . . . **30** B1
Pondgate MK7 . . . . **30** B2
Poplar Cl
  Leighton Buzzard LU7 . . . . . . **66** A4

Poplar Cl continued
  Milton Keynes MK6 . . . . **36** C3
Poplars Rd MK18 . . . . **74** C4
Porlock La MK4 . . . . **34** A2
Portchester Ct **1** MK8 . . . . . **25** C3
Porter's Cl MK19 . . . . **14** C2
Portfield Cl MK18 . . . . **75** A4
Port Field Farm MK16 . . . . **2** B3
Portfields Comb Sch MK16 . . . . **2** C3
Portfields Rd MK16 . . . . **3** A2
Portfield Way MK18 . . . . **75** A4
Porthcawl Gn MK3 . . . . **44** A2
Porthleven Pl MK6 . . . . **28** A4
Porthmellin Cl MK4 . . . . **43** C2
Portishead Dr MK4 . . . . **43** A2
Portland Dr MK15 . . . . **12** B1
Portmarnock Cl MK3 . . . . **44** B2
Portrush Cl MK3 . . . . **44** B2
Portway
  Milton Keynes,Bradwell
  Common MK5,MK9,MK13,MK14,
  MK15 . . . . **27** A4
  Milton Keynes,Shenley Church End
  MK8,MK5 . . . . **33** A4
Portway Rdbt MK5 . . . . **26** B3
Potters La MK11 . . . . **17** C2
Poundfield Rd NN12 . . . . **5** A4
Pound Hill MK17 . . . . **59** B3
Powell Haven MK10 . . . . **22** C1
Powis La MK4 . . . . **43** A4
Precedent Dr MK13 . . . . **19** C1
Prentice Gr MK5 . . . . **33** C1
Presley Way MK8 . . . . **25** B1
Preston Ct MK15 . . . . **12** A1
Prestwick Cl MK3 . . . . **44** B1
Primatt Cres MK5 . . . . **33** C4
Primrose Rd MK13 . . . . **19** B2
Primrose Way MK18 . . . . **74** B3
Princes Ct LU7 . . . . **65** C2
Princes Way MK2 . . . . **46** A2
Princes Way Rdbt MK2 . . . . . . **45** C2
Priors Pk MK4 . . . . **44** B4
Priory Cl MK16 . . . . **4** A2
Priory Common Fst Sch
  MK13 . . . . **19** C2
Priory St MK16 . . . . **4** A2
Pritchard Ct MK14 . . . . **11** A2
Proctor Rise MK8 . . . . **32** B4
Prospect Rd MK11 . . . . **16** A3
Protheroe Field MK7 . . . . **38** B2
Providence Pl MK13 . . . . **19** B2
Pulborough Cl MK3 . . . . **44** B3
Pulford Rd LU7 . . . . **69** C4
Pulford's Lower Sch LU7 . . . . **70** A4
Purbeck MK13 . . . . **20** A4
Purcel Dr MK16 . . . . **3** B1
Purwell Wlk LU7 . . . . **63** A1
Putman Ho MK5 . . . . **34** A3
Puxley Rd MK19 . . . . **14** B3
Pyke Hayes MK8 . . . . **18** B1
Pyxe Ct MK7 . . . . **37** B2

Q

Quadrans Cl MK15 . . . . **11** C1
Quantock Cres MK4 . . . . **44** B4
Queen Anne St MK13 . . . . **9** B1
Queen Eleanor Combined Sch
  MK11 . . . . **17** A2
Queen Eleanor St MK11 . . . . . **16** C4
Queens Ave MK16 . . . . **3** B2
Queensbury La MK10 . . . . **29** B3
Queen St
  Leighton Buzzard LU7 . . . . . . **65** C2
  Milton Keynes MK11 . . . . **16** C4
Queensway Bletchley MK2 . . . **46** A2
  Milton Keynes MK2 . . . . **46** B2
Quilter Mdw MK7 . . . . **38** B3
Quince Cl MK7 . . . . **37** C3
Quinton Dr MK13 . . . . **19** C1

R

Rackstraw Gr MK7 . . . . **38** B3

Radcliffe Sch The MK12 . . . . . . **17** C4
Radcliffe St MK12 . . . . **18** B4
Radcote Lodge MK8 . . . . **25** B3
Radian Ct MK5 . . . . **26** C1
Radman Gr MK12 . . . . **17** C3
Radworthy MK4 . . . . **34** A1
Raglan Dr MK4 . . . . **42** C3
Rainbow Dr MK6 . . . . **27** C1
Rainsborough MK14 . . . . **11** C2
Ramsay Cl MK13 . . . . **19** C1
Ramsgill Ct MK13 . . . . **20** A3
Ramsons Ave MK14 . . . . **20** C2
Ramsthorn Gr MK7 . . . . **37** C4
Randolph Cl MK13 . . . . **19** B4
Ranelagh Gdns MK16 . . . . **12** B4
Rangers Ct MK8 . . . . **25** C3
Rannoch Cl MK2 . . . . **55** A3
Rannock Gdns LU7 . . . . **64** C1
Rashleigh Pl MK6 . . . . **27** B1
Rathbone Cl MK8 . . . . **25** B1
Ravel Cl MK7 . . . . **38** B4
Ravensbourne Pl MK6 . . . . **28** B4
Ravenscar Ct MK4 . . . . **44** A4
Ravensglass Croft MK10 . . . . . **23** C1
Ravigill Pl MK12 . . . . **18** B2
Rawlins Rd MK13 . . . . **19** B2
Rayleigh Cl MK5 . . . . **33** C4
Rayners La MK9 . . . . **29** B3
Reach Gn LU7 . . . . **62** C4
Reach La LU7 . . . . **63** A3
Rectory Fields MK15 . . . . **22** B1
Redbourne Ct MK11 . . . . **17** A3
Redbridge MK14 . . . . **10** C1
Redcote Manor MK7 . . . . **37** B2
Redding Gr MK8 . . . . **32** C4
Red House Ct MK17 . . . . **53** A2
Redhuish Cl MK4 . . . . **34** B1
Redland Dr MK5 . . . . **26** C1
Redshaw Cl MK18 . . . . **71** A1
Redvers Gate MK15 . . . . **12** A1
Redway Sch The MK6 . . . . **36** A4
Redwood Gate MK5 . . . . **34** A2
Redwood Glade
  Leighton Buzzard LU7 . . . . . . **62** B1
  Leighton Buzzard LU7 . . . . . . **62** C1
Reeves Croft MK12 . . . . **18** A2
Regents Hall MK11 . . . . **16** C3
Regent St
  Leighton Buzzard LU7 . . . . . . **66** B1
  Milton Keynes MK2 . . . . **46** A2
Reliance La MK9 . . . . **21** C1
Rendlesham MK15 . . . . **22** A1
Renfrew Way MK3 . . . . **35** A1
Retreat The MK11 . . . . **16** B3
Reynolds Pl MK8 . . . . **32** B4
Rhodes Pl MK6 . . . . **27** B1
Rhondda Cl MK1 . . . . **46** C3
Rhoscolyn Dr MK3 . . . . **44** A2
Rhuddlan Cl MK5 . . . . **25** C1
Ribble Cl MK16 . . . . **4** A2
Ribble Cres MK3 . . . . **44** B2
Richardson Pl **2** MK6 . . . . . . **27** B3
Richborough MK13 . . . . **19** B4
Richmond Cl MK3 . . . . **44** B3
Richmond Rd LU7 . . . . **70** C4
Richmond Way MK16 . . . . **3** C1
Rickley La MK3 . . . . **45** B2
Rickley Mid Sch MK3 . . . . **45** A2
Rickyard Ct MK13 . . . . **19** B2
Ridgeway
  Milton Keynes,Stony Stratford
  MK11 . . . . **17** A2
  Milton Keynes,Wolverton Mill
  MK12 . . . . **17** B3
Ridgmont Cl MK19 . . . . **14** C3
Ridgmont MK19 . . . . **14** C3
Ridgway MK17 . . . . **39** C4
Riding The MK19 . . . . **14** C3
Rillington Gdns MK4 . . . . **33** C1
Rimsdale Cl MK2 . . . . **55** A1
Ring Rd E MK7 . . . . **29** C1
Ring Rd N MK7 . . . . **29** C1

Ring Rd W MK7 . . . . 29 B1
Ripley Cl MK4 . . . . 42 C3
River Cl MK16 . . . . 3 C2
Rivercrest Rd MK19. . . . . 15 C4
Rivers Fst Sch MK3 . . . . 44 C3
Riverside MK16 . . . . 4 A1
Riverside Fst Sch MK16 . . . . 4 A1
Riverside MK7 . . . . 66 A2
Riverside Mews MK18. . . . . 74 C4
River Side MK16 . . . . 3 C2
Rixband Cl MK7 . . . . 37 C2
Roberts Cl MK19 . . . . 14 C2
Robertson Ct MK5 . . . . 25 C1
Robeson Pl MK8 . . . . 25 B2
Robin Cl MK8 . . . . 75 B3
Robins Hill MK6 . . . . 35 B4
Robinswood Cl LU7 . . . . 65 C4
Roche Gdns MK3 . . . . 45 B2
Rochester Ct MK5 . . . . 33 B3
Rochester Mews LU7 . . . . 69 B4
Rochfords MK6 . . . . 35 A4
Rock Cl LU7 . . . . 69 A4
Rockingham Dr MK14. . . . . 20 C4
Rock La LU7 . . . . 65 A1
Rockleigh Ct **3** LU7 . . . . 65 B1
Rockspray Gr MK7 . . . . 37 C3
Rodwell Gdns MK7 . . . . 38 B2
Roebuck Way MK5 . . . . 34 A4
Roeburn Cres MK4. . . . . 44 A3
Rogers Croft MK6 . . . . 29 A1
Rolvenden Gr MK7. . . . . 30 B1
Romans Field Sch MK3 . . . . . . 44 C3
Romar Ct MK1. . . . . 46 A4
Rooksley Rdbt MK13 . . . . 19 C1
Roosevelt Ave LU7 . . . . 66 B2
Ropa Ct **6** LU7 . . . . 65 C1
Rosebay Cl MK7 . . . . 37 C3
Rosebery Ave LU7 . . . . 65 B1
Rosebery Ct **4** LU7 . . . . 65 C1
Rosecomb Pl MK5 . . . . 33 B2
Rosemary Ct MK7. . . . . 37 B3
Rosemullion Ave MK4. . . . . 43 C2
Roslyn Ct MK15. . . . . 12 C1
Rossal Pl MK12 . . . . 18 B2
Rossendale MK14. . . . . 10 C1
Rossini Pl MK7 . . . . 38 B3
Ross Way MK3. . . . . 45 A4
Rothersthorpe MK14. . . . . 11 C2
Rothschild Rd LU7. . . . . 65 C2
Rotten Row MK17. . . . . 59 B4
Roundel Dr LU7 . . . . 71 A3
Roveley Ct MK11. . . . . 17 A3
Rowan Dr MK19 . . . . 8 C4
Rowlands Cl MK2. . . . . 46 C2
Rowle Cl MK14 . . . . 11 A1
Rowley Furrows LU7. . . . . 65 A2
Rowsham Dell MK14. . . . . 11 B4
Rowton Heath MK5. . . . . 32 A3
Roxburgh Way MK3. . . . . 35 A1
Royal Latin Sch MK18. . . . . 74 C3
Rubbra Cl MK7 . . . . 38 A3
Rudchesters MK13. . . . . 19 A3
Runford Ct MK5 . . . . 34 A3
Runnymede MK14 . . . . 11 B4
Rushfields Cl MK4 . . . . 43 A3
Rushleys Cl MK5. . . . . 26 A2
Rushmere Cl MK17 . . . . 48 B4
Rushmere Ret Pk MK1. . . . . . . 46 B4
Rushton Ct **5** MK8 . . . . 25 C2
Ruskin Ct MK16. . . . . 12 B4
Rusland Cir MK4. . . . . 44 A4
Russell Fst Sch MK11. . . . . 16 B3
Russell St
  Milton Keynes MK11. . . . . 16 B3
  Woburn Sands MK17 . . . . 39 C2
Russell Way LU7 . . . . 67 A1
Russwell La MK17 . . . . 56 C4
Rutherford Gate MK5 . . . . 34 A3
Ruthven Ct MK2 . . . . 54 C2
Rutland Ho **3** MK3 . . . . 45 A3
Rycroft MK4 . . . . 34 C1
Rydal Way MK2. . . . . 55 A3
Ryding The MK5 . . . . 33 B2

Rye Cl LU7 . . . . 67 A1
Ryeland MK11 . . . . 16 C4
Rylands Mews LU7. . . . . 70 A4
Rylstone Cl MK13 . . . . 19 C1
Ryton Pl MK4. . . . . 34 A1

S

Saddington MK6. . . . . 36 B4
Saddlers Pl MK14 . . . . 21 B3
Sadleirs Gn MK17. . . . . 39 C3
Saffron St MK2 . . . . 46 B1
St Abbs Cl MK4 . . . . 43 A2
St Aidan's Cl MK3. . . . . 53 B4
St Andrew's CE Fst Sch
  MK14. 11 A2
St Andrews Cl LU7 . . . . 66 A1
St Andrew's Rd MK3 . . . . 44 C1
St Andrew's St LU7 . . . . 66 A2
St Anthony's Pl MK4 . . . . 43 C2
St Bartholomews MK10 . . . . . . 30 A3
St Bees MK10. . . . . 30 B3
St Botolphs **2** MK10. . . . . 30 B3
St Brides Cl MK6. . . . . 28 C4
St Catherine's Ave MK3 . . . . . . 53 A4
St Clement's Dr MK3. . . . . 53 A4
St David's Rd MK3 . . . . 53 B4
St Dunstans MK6 . . . . 35 B4
St Edwards Ct MK14 . . . . 11 B1
St Faith's Cl MK17 . . . . 53 A1
St George's Cl LU7. . . . . 66 B2
St George's Lower Sch LU7 66 B2
St George's Rd MK3 . . . . 53 B4
St Georges Way. 8 C1
St Giles Mews MK11 . . . . 16 B4
St Giles St MK13. . . . . 9 B1
St Govans Cl MK4. . . . . 43 C2
St Helens Gr MK10. . . . . 29 C2
St Ives Cres MK4. . . . . 43 C2
St James St MK13 . . . . 9 B1
St John's Cres MK12. . . . . 18 B3
St John's Rd MK3. . . . . 53 B4
St John's Terr MK16. . . . . 3 C2
St John St MK16 . . . . 3 C2
St Lawrence View MK13 . . . . . . 19 B2
St Leger Ct MK14 . . . . 11 A2
St Leger Dr MK14 . . . . 11 A1
St Leonard's Cl LU7 . . . . 63 A1
St Leonard's-Heath and Reach
  Lower Sch LU7 . . . . 62 C3
St Margaret Ct MK2. . . . . 46 C2
St Margarets Cl MK16. . . . . 4 A2
St Martin's St MK2. . . . . 46 A2
St Mary Magdalene RC Comb
  Sch MK12 . . . . 17 B3
St Mary & St Giles CE Mid
  Sch MK11 . . . . 16 C4
St Mary's Ave
  Milton Keynes MK3. . . . . 44 C1
  Milton Keynes,Stony Stratford
  MK11. . . . . 16 C4
St Mary's Cl MK17 . . . . 31 B1
St Mary St MK13 . . . . 9 B1
St Mary's Way LU7. . . . . 65 A1
St Matthews Ct MK3 . . . . 53 B4
St Michaels Dr
  Milton Keynes MK7. . . . . 37 A4
  Walton MK7 . . . . 29 B1
St Monica's RC Comb Sch
  MK14. 21 A4
St Patrick's Way MK3 . . . . 53 B4
St Pauls Ct MK11 . . . . 16 B4
St Pauls RC Sch MK6. . . . . 27 C1
St Paul's Rd MK3 . . . . 53 B4
St Pauls Yd MK16 . . . . 3 C2
St Peters Way MK13 . . . . 9 C2
St Rumbold's La MK18 . . . . . . 74 B4
St Stephens Dr MK15 . . . . 12 A1
St Thomas Aquinas RC Comb
  Sch MK13 . . . . 44 C1
St Thomas Ct MK4. . . . . 43 A3
St Vincents MK17 . . . . 40 A2
Salden Ct MK5. . . . . 33 C4
Salisbury Gr MK14 . . . . 11 B4
Salop Ho MK3 . . . . 45 A4

Salters Mews MK14. . . . . 21 A4
Salton Link MK4 . . . . 43 C4
Saltwood Ave MK4. . . . . 42 C3
Samphire Ct MK7 . . . . 37 B4
Samuel Cl MK16 . . . . 4 B1
Sandal Ct MK5. . . . . 33 B3
Sandbrier Cl MK7. . . . . 37 C4
Sandhills LU7 . . . . 66 B3
Sandhurst Dr MK18 . . . . 74 B3
Sandown Ct MK3 . . . . 53 A4
Sandringham Ct MK16 . . . . 3 A1
Sandringham Pl MK2 . . . . 46 A2
Sandwell Ct MK8 . . . . 24 C4
Sandy Cl Buckingham MK18 . . 75 B4
  Milton Keynes MK14. . . . . 10 C2
Sandy La Aspley Heath MK17 . . 49 C4
  Leighton Buzzard LU7. . . . . . . 62 B1
  Leighton Buzzard LU7. . . . . . . 62 C1
Sandywell Dr MK15 . . . . 21 B4
San Remo Rd MK17 . . . . 41 A2
Santen Gr MK2 . . . . 55 A2
Saracens' Wharf MK2. . . . . 46 C3
Saturn Ct LU7 . . . . 67 A2
Saunders Ct MK7 . . . . 38 B4
Savage Croft MK10 . . . . 22 C1
Savill La MK4,MK5. . . . . 43 A4
Savoy Cres MK9 . . . . 21 A1
Sawley Ho **5** MK3 . . . . 45 A3
Saxon Gate MK9. . . . . 27 B4
Saxons Cl LU7 . . . . 66 C1
Saxon St
  Milton Keynes,Ashland MK1,
  MK6. 36 A2
  Milton Keynes,Heelands MK6,
  MK13,MK14. . . . . 20 A3
  Milton Keynes MK2. . . . . 46 A2
Scardale MK13 . . . . 20 A3
Scatterill Cl MK13 . . . . 19 B2
School Dr MK17 . . . . 52 C1
School La Buckingham MK18 . . 74 B4
  Husborne Crawley MK43 . . . . 41 C2
  Milton Keynes MK5. . . . . 26 B2
School St MK13. . . . . 9 B1
Schumann Cl MK7 . . . . 38 A2
Scotch Firs MK7 . . . . 38 A4
Scotney Gdns MK3. . . . . 44 C2
Scott Dr MK16 . . . . 2 C3
Scotts Cl MK17 . . . . 58 A2
Scotts Cl MK17. . . . . 58 A2
Scotts Farm Ct MK18. . . . . 71 A4
Scotts La MK18 . . . . 71 A3
Scriven Ct MK15 . . . . 13 A1
Seabrooke Ct MK8. . . . . 32 B4
Seagrave Ct MK7 . . . . 37 B2
Secklow Gate MK9. . . . . 21 A1
Second Ave MK1. . . . . 46 A4
Sedgemere MK8. . . . . 24 A4
Selbourne Ave MK3. . . . . 45 A1
Selby Gr MK5. . . . . 33 C3
Selkirk Gr MK3 . . . . 45 A4
Selworthy MK4 . . . . 34 B1
Serjeants Gn MK14 . . . . 21 A4
Serles Cl MK6 . . . . 35 B4
Serpentine Ct MK2. . . . . 55 A3
Severn Dr MK16 . . . . 4 A2
Severn Way MK3 . . . . 44 B2
Severn Wlk LU7 . . . . 63 A1
Shackleton Pl MK6 . . . . 27 B3
Shaftesbury Cres MK3 . . . . 45 B3
Shakespeare Cl MK16. . . . . 2 C3
Shallowford Gr MK4 . . . . 34 B2
Shamrock Cl MK7 . . . . 37 C4
Shannon Ct MK14. . . . . 21 B4
Sharkham Ct MK4 . . . . 43 C3
Sharman Wlk MK13 . . . . 19 B1
Shaw Cl MK16 . . . . 2 C3
Shearmans MK11 . . . . 17 B2
Sheelin Gr MK2. . . . . 55 A2
Sheepcoat Cl MK5 . . . . 33 B3
Sheepcote Cres LU7 . . . . 62 C3
Sheering Gr MK13 . . . . 10 A2
Sheerness Ct MK4 . . . . 43 B2
Sheldon Ct MK8 . . . . 25 C3
Shelley Cl MK16 . . . . 3 A2
Shelley Dr MK3 . . . . 45 A1

Shelsmore MK14 . . . . 11 C3
Shelton Ct MK17. . . . . 39 C2
Shenley Brook End Sch
  MK5. . . . . 43 B4
Shenley Cl LU7 . . . . 63 A1
Shenley Hill Rd LU7. . . . . 63 B1
Shenley Rdbt MK5 . . . . 33 B3
Shenley Rd
  Milton Keynes,Bletchley
  MK3. 44 C3
  Milton Keynes,Bletchley MK3. . . 45 A2
  Milton Keynes,Loughton MK5. . . 26 A1
  Whaddon MK17 . . . . 42 A2
Shepherds Mead LU7 . . . . 66 A3
Shepherds MK11 . . . . 17 B2
Shepherdswell Fst Sch
  MK6. . . . . 28 B4
Sheppards Cl MK16 . . . . 3 B2
Shepperds Gn MK5 . . . . 33 A4
Sherbourne Dr MK7 . . . . 37 C2
Shernfold MK7 . . . . 30 B1
Sherwood Dr MK1,MK2,MK3. . 45 C3
Shilling Cl MK15. . . . . 11 C1
Shipley Rd MK16. . . . . 3 A2
Shipman Ct MK15. . . . . 12 A1
Ship Rd LU7 . . . . 69 B4
Shipton Hill MK13 . . . . 19 C4
Shire Ct MK14 . . . . 21 B3
Shirley Moor MK7. . . . . 30 B2
Shirwell Cres MK4 . . . . 34 B3
Shorham Rise MK8 . . . . 25 B4
Shouler Cl MK5. . . . . 33 B3
Shrewsbury Cl MK10. . . . . 30 A4
Shropshire Ct MK3. . . . . 44 C3
Shuttleworth Gr MK7 . . . . 38 B4
Sidlow Ct MK11. . . . . 17 A2
Silbury Arc MK9 . . . . 20 C1
Silbury Bvd MK9. . . . . 27 A4
Silbury Rdbt MK9 . . . . 26 C3
Silicon Ct MK5 . . . . 34 A3
Silverbirches La MK17 . . . . 49 B4
Silver St Milton Keynes MK11. . 16 B3
  Newport Pagnell MK16 . . . . . . 3 C2
Silverweed Ct MK7 . . . . 37 C3
Simms Croft MK10. . . . . 30 A4
Simnel MK6 . . . . 35 C4
Simonsbath MK4 . . . . 44 B4
Simons Lea MK13. . . . . 19 C2
Simpson Comb Sch MK6. . . . . 36 B3
Simpson Dr MK6 . . . . 36 C3
Simpson Rdbt MK6 . . . . 36 B3
Simpson Rd MK1,MK2,MK6 . . 36 C1
Sinclair Ct MK1. . . . . 35 C1
Singleton Dr MK8. . . . . 32 B4
Sipthorp Cl MK7 . . . . 38 A4
Sir Frank Markham Com Coll
  MK6. . . . . 27 C1
Sir Frank Markham Com Sch
  MK6. . . . . 28 A1
Sissinghurst Dr MK4 . . . . 42 C4
Sitwell Cl MK16. . . . . 2 B3
Skeats Wharf MK15 . . . . 11 C1
Skeldon Gate MK14 . . . . 21 B2
Skeldon Rdbt MK9. . . . . 21 B2
Skene Cl MK2 . . . . 54 C2
Skipton Cl MK15 . . . . 22 A4
Slade La MK11. . . . . 17 B2
Slade The MK17 . . . . 53 A1
Slated Row MK12 . . . . 8 A1
Slated Row Sch MK12 . . . . 7 C1
Smabridge Wlk MK15. . . . . 12 C1
Small Cres MK18 . . . . 75 B4
Smarden Bell MK7. . . . . 30 B2
Smeaton Cl MK14. . . . . 11 C4
Smithergill Ct MK13 . . . . 20 A3
Smithsons Pl MK9 . . . . 21 C1
Snaith Cres MK5. . . . . 26 B1
Snelshall St MK4 . . . . 43 A2
Snowberry Cl MK12. . . . . 18 B3
Snowdon Dr MK6. . . . . 27 A1
Snowshill Ct MK14. . . . . 11 B4
Sokeman Cl MK12 . . . . 17 B3
Solar Ct MK14 . . . . 11 A3
Somerset Cl MK3. . . . . 45 A3
Sorensen Ct MK5 . . . . 32 C2

Sorrell Dr MK16 . . . . 2 B2
Soskin Dr MK14 . . . . 20 B4
Soulbury Rd LU7 . . . . 65 A1
Southbridge Gr MK7 . . . . 30 A1
Southcott Lower Sch LU7. . . 65 A2
Southcott Village LU7. . . . . . 69 A4
Southcourt Ave LU7 . . . . 69 A4
Southcourt Ho LU7 . . . . 65 A1
Southcourt Rd LU7 . . . . 65 A1
South Eighth St MK9 . . . . . . 27 B4
South Enmore Rdbt MK6. . . 21 C1
Southern Way MK12 . . . . 18 B3
Southfield Cl MK15 . . . . 13 A1
South Fifth St MK9 . . . . 27 B3
South Fourth St MK9 . . . . . . 27 A3
South Hall MK18. . . . . 71 A3
South Ho MK1. . . . . 36 B1
South Lawne MK3 . . . . 45 A2
South Ninth St MK9. . . . . . . 27 C4
South Overgate Rdbt MK6. . 21 C1
South Row
  Milton Keynes MK9. . . . . 27 B3
  Milton Keynes MK9. . . . . 27 C4
South Saxon Rdbt MK9 . . . . . 27 C3
South Secklow Rdbt MK6 . . 27 C4
South Second St MK9 . . . . . . 27 A3
South Seventh St MK9 . . . . . 27 B3
South Sixth St MK9 . . . . 27 B3
South St LU7 . . . . 66 B1
South Tenth St MK9 . . . . 27 C4
South Terr MK2. . . . . 46 A2
Southview Gdns LU7 . . . . 70 B4
Southwick Ct MK8 . . . . 25 C2
South Witan Rdbt MK6 . . . . . 27 B3
Southwood Mid Sch MK14. . 20 C3
Sovereign Dr MK15 . . . . 11 C1
Sovereign Lodge MK15 . . . . . 11 C1
Spark Way MK16. . . . . 2 B3
Sparsholt Cl MK4 . . . . 44 A4
Spearmint Cl MK7 . . . . 37 C3
Specklands MK5. . . . . 26 A2
Speedwell Pl MK14 . . . . 20 C2
Speldhurst Ct MK7. . . . . 30 B1
Spencer Ct LU7. . . . . 66 B3
Spencer MK14. . . . . 10 B2
Spencer St MK13 . . . . 9 B1
Spenlows Rd MK3 . . . . 35 B1
Spinney La MK17 . . . . 41 A2
Spinney The MK13 . . . . 19 B2
Spoonley Wood MK13. . . . . . 18 C3
Springfield Bvd MK6. . . . . . . 28 B4
Springfield Ct
  1 Leighton Buzzard LU7. . . . . 65 B1
  Milton Keynes MK6. . . . . 28 B4
Springfield Gdns MK19 . . . . 14 C2
Springfield Mid Sch MK6 . . 28 B4
Springfield Rdbt MK6. . . . . . 28 A4
Springfield Rd LU7 . . . . 65 B1
Spring Gdns MK16 . . . . 3 B2
Spring Gr MK17. . . . . 39 C3
Springside 2 LU7 . . . . 65 B1
Square The
  Aspley Guise MK17. . . . . 40 C2
  Milton Keynes MK12. . . . . 18 B4
Squires Cl MK6. . . . . 35 B4
Squirrels Way MK18 . . . . 75 A3
Stacey Ave MK12 . . . . 18 B4
Stacey Bushes Trad Ctr
  MK12. . . . . 18 C2
Stafford Gr MK5 . . . . 33 C4
Stagshaw Gr 5 MK4 . . . . . . 43 C4
Stainton Dr MK13. . . . . 20 A2
Stamford Ave MK6. . . . . 28 B4
Stanbridge Ct MK11 . . . . 17 A3
Stanbridge Rd LU7 . . . . 70 B4
Stanbridge Road Terr LU7. . 70 B4
Stanbrook Pl MK10 . . . . 30 A3
Standing Way
  Milton Keynes,Coldharbour
    Spinney MK3,MK4. . . . . 34 C1
  Milton Keynes,Kingston
    MK10. . . . . 30 C3
  Milton Keynes,Peartree Bridge
    MK10,MK4,MK6 . . . . 28 C1

Standing Way continued
  Milton Keynes,Snelshall East
    MK4. . . . . 43 C1
Stanier Sq 5 MK2 . . . . 46 A2
Stanmore Gdns MK16. . . . . . 12 A4
Stanton Ave MK13 . . . . 19 B4
Stantonbury Campus MK14 . 10 B1
Stantonbury Cl MK13 . . . . . . 9 C2
Stanton Gate MK14 . . . . 10 C2
Stanton Mid Sch MK13. . . . . 10 A1
Stanton Wood Rdbt MK14. . 20 B2
Stanway Cl MK15 . . . . 21 C4
Stapeley Ct MK4 . . . . 43 A4
Staple Hall Rd MK1. . . . . 46 C3
Staters Pound MK15 . . . . . . 11 C1
Statham Pl MK6 . . . . 27 C2
Station Rd
  Bow Brickhill MK17 . . . . 48 A4
  Buckingham MK18 . . . . 74 B3
  Leighton Buzzard LU7. . . . . . . 65 B1
  Newport Pagnell MK16 . . . . . . 3 B2
  Woburn Sands MK17 . . . . 39 C3
Station Sq MK9 . . . . 26 C3
Station Terr
  Buckingham MK18 . . . . 74 B3
  Milton Keynes MK11 . . . . 11 A4
Staunton Ho MK17. . . . . 51 A1
Stavordale 2 MK10. . . . . 30 A3
Stayning La MK14. . . . . 21 A4
Steeple Cl MK4 . . . . 43 B2
Steinbeck Cres MK4 . . . . 43 A1
Stephenson Cl LU7 . . . . 69 B4
Steppingstone Pl LU7. . . . . . 70 B4
Stevens Field MK7 . . . . 38 B4
Stile The LU7 . . . . 62 C3
Stirling Cl MK15 . . . . 21 B4
Stirling Ho MK3 . . . . 44 B1
Stockdale MK13 . . . . 20 A3
Stocks The MK19 . . . . 7 A4
Stockwell La MK17 . . . . 31 A1
Stoke La MK17. . . . . 59 B3
Stokenchurch Pl MK13 . . . . 20 A1
Stoke Rd
  Leighton Buzzard LU7. . . . . . . 65 A3
  Milton Keynes MK2. . . . . 55 B3
  Newton Longville MK17 . . . . . 53 C1
Stokesay Ct MK4 . . . . 42 C4
Stolford Rise MK4 . . . . 43 C3
Stonebridge Rdbt MK13. . . . 9 A2
Stonecrop Pl MK14 . . . . 20 C2
Stonegate MK13 . . . . 19 B3
Stone Hill MK8 . . . . 25 A3
Stoneleigh Ct MK4. . . . . 42 C3
Stonor Ct MK8. . . . . 25 C2
Stony Stratford Nature
  Reserve ★ MK11,MK19 . . . . . . 6 C1
Stotfold Ct MK11 . . . . 16 C2
Stour Cl Milton Keynes MK3 . . 44 C2
  Newport Pagnell MK16 . . . . . . 4 A1
Stourhead Gate MK4. . . . . . . 42 C4
Stowe Ave MK18. . . . . 72 A3
Stowe Cl MK18 . . . . 72 B1
Stowe Ct MK14 . . . . 10 B2
Stowe Rise MK18 . . . . 72 B1
Strangford Dr MK2 . . . . 54 C2
Stratfield Ct MK8 . . . . 25 C3
Stratford Arc MK11 . . . . 16 B4
Stratford Rd
  Buckingham MK18 . . . . 71 A1
  Cosgrove MK19 . . . . 6 C3
  Deanshanger MK19 . . . . 15 A2
  Milton Keynes MK12. . . . . 8 B1
  Old Stratford MK19 . . . . 15 C3
Strathnaver Pl MK12. . . . . . . 18 B2
Stratton Mews LU7 . . . . 66 B1
Strauss Gr MK7 . . . . 38 A2
Streatham Pl MK13 . . . . 26 C4
Strudwick Dr MK6 . . . . 27 C2
Stuart Cl MK2 . . . . 46 B3
Stubbs Field MK5. . . . . 33 B1
Studley Knapp MK7. . . . . 30 B1
Sturges Cl MK7 . . . . 37 B3
Sudgrove Ho MK15 . . . . 21 B4
Suffolk Cl MK3 . . . . 45 A3
Sulgrave Ct 3 MK8. . . . . 25 C2

Sullivan Cres MK7 . . . . 38 A3
Sultan Croft MK5 . . . . 33 B2
Summerfield Comb Sch
  MK13. . . . . 20 A1
Summergill Ct MK13 . . . . . . 20 A3
Summerhayes MK14 . . . . 11 B1
Summerson Ct MK6 . . . . 35 A3
Summerson Rd
  Bleak Hall MK6. . . . . 35 B3
  Milton Keynes MK6. . . . . 35 A3
Summer St LU7. . . . . 66 B1
Sumner Ct MK5. . . . . 26 A2
Sunbury Cl MK13 . . . . 19 B4
Sunderland Ct MK4 . . . . 43 A3
Sunningdale Way MK3 . . . . . 44 B2
Sunridge Cl MK16 . . . . 3 B1
Sunrise Parkway MK14. . . . . 20 C4
Sunset Cl MK2. . . . . 46 A1
Sunset Wlk MK9 . . . . 27 B4
Surrey Pl MK3 . . . . 45 A4
Surrey Rd MK3 . . . . 45 A4
Sussex Rd MK3 . . . . 45 A3
Sutcliffe Ave MK6. . . . . 27 B3
Sutherland Gr MK3 . . . . 35 A1
Sutleye Ct MK5 . . . . 33 B3
Sutton Cl MK4 . . . . 44 A3
Swales Dr LU7. . . . . 71 A4
Swallow Cl MK18 . . . . 75 A3
Swallowfield Lower Sch
  MK17. . . . . 39 C3
Swallowfield MK8 . . . . 25 B3
Swan Cl MK18 . . . . 75 A3
Swan Ct LU7 . . . . 69 B4
Swan Terr MK11 . . . . 16 B3
Swanwick La MK10 . . . . 23 C1
Swayne Rise MK10. . . . . 30 A4
Sweetlands Cnr MK7. . . . . . . 30 B2
Swift Cl MK16 . . . . 2 C3
Swimbridge La MK4 . . . . 34 B2
Swinden Ct MK13. . . . . 19 C2
Sycamore Ave MK2 . . . . 46 C2
Sycamore Cl MK18. . . . . 75 B3
Sykes Croft MK4 . . . . 44 A3
Sylvester St LU7 . . . . 62 C3
Symington Ct MK5. . . . . 33 C3
Syon Gdns MK16. . . . . 12 B4

T

Tabard Gdns MK16. . . . . 12 B4
Tacknell Dr MK5. . . . . 33 B2
Tadmarton MK15 . . . . 21 B4
Tadmere MK8 . . . . 25 A3
Talbot Ct
  Leighton Buzzard LU7. . . . . . . 66 A2
  Milton Keynes MK15. . . . . 28 C3
Talland Ave MK6 . . . . 27 C3
Tallis La MK7 . . . . 38 A3
Tall Pines LU7 . . . . 65 C4
Tamar Ho MK3. . . . . 44 C3
Tamarisk Ct MK7 . . . . 37 C3
Tamar Wlk LU7 . . . . 63 A1
Tamworth Stubb MK7. . . . . . 37 B3
Tandra MK6 . . . . 35 C3
Tanfield La MK10 . . . . 23 B1
Tanners Dr MK14 . . . . 11 C4
Tansman La MK7 . . . . 38 B3
Taranis Cl MK7 . . . . 30 C1
Tarbert Ct MK2 . . . . 54 C3
Tarnbrook Cl 6 MK4. . . . . . 43 C4
Tarragon Cl MK7 . . . . 37 B4
Tatling Gr MK7 . . . . 37 B4
Tattam Cl MK15. . . . . 28 C4
Tattenhoe La MK3 . . . . 44 B2
Tattenhoe St MK5. . . . . 32 C2
Tattershall Cl MK5. . . . . 33 B4
Taunton Deane MK4 . . . . 44 B4
Tavelhurst MK8. . . . . 25 B3
Taverner Cl MK7. . . . . 38 B3
Tavistock Cl MK17 . . . . 39 C4
Tavistock St MK2 . . . . 46 B3
Taylors Mews MK14. . . . . 21 A4
Taylor's Ride LU7. . . . . 65 C4
Taymouth Pl MK9 . . . . 21 C1
Tay Rd MK3. . . . . 44 C3

Teasel Ave MK14. . . . . 20 C3
Tees Way MK3 . . . . 44 B3
Teign Cl MK16 . . . . 3 C2
Telford Way MK14 . . . . 12 A3
Temperance Terr MK11 . . . . 16 A4
Temple Cl Buckingham MK18. . 71 A2
  Milton Keynes MK3. . . . . 44 B1
Temple MK14. . . . . 10 B1
Tenby Gr MK4 . . . . 42 B3
Tene Acres MK5 . . . . 33 A4
Tennant Cl MK8 . . . . 32 B4
Tennyson Dr MK16. . . . . 2 C2
Tennyson Gr MK3 . . . . 45 A1
Tenterden Cres MK7 . . . . . . 30 B1
Terrace The MK17. . . . . 40 C3
Tewkesbury La MK10. . . . . . . 29 C3
Thames Cl MK3. . . . . 44 C2
Thames Dr MK16 . . . . 4 A1
Thane Ct MK14 . . . . 10 B1
Theatre Wlk MK9 . . . . 21 A1
Theydon Ave MK17 . . . . 39 C2
Third Ave MK1. . . . . 45 C4
Thirlby La MK5 . . . . 33 B4
Thirlmere Ave MK2 . . . . 55 A4
Thirsk Gdns MK3 . . . . 52 C4
Thomas Dr MK16 . . . . 2 C4
Thomas St LU7 . . . . 62 C3
Thompson St MK13 . . . . 9 C1
Thorncliffe MK8 . . . . 25 A3
Thorneycroft La MK15 . . . . . 21 C3
Thornley Croft MK4. . . . . 44 A4
Thorpeness Croft MK4 . . . . . 43 A2
Thorwold Pl MK5 . . . . 33 C4
Thresher Gr MK12 . . . . 17 B3
Threshers Ct LU7 . . . . 67 A1
Thrift Rd LU7. . . . . 62 C3
Thurne Cl MK16 . . . . 4 A1
Thursby Cl MK15 . . . . 12 C1
Thyme Cl MK16. . . . . 2 B3
Ticehirst Cl MK7. . . . . 30 B1
Ticehurst Cl MK7 . . . . 30 B1
Tickford Arc MK16 . . . . 3 C2
Tickford St MK16 . . . . 4 A2
Tidbury Cl MK17 . . . . 39 B2
Tiddenfoot Waterside Pk★
  LU7. 69 B2
Tiffany Cl MK16 . . . . 2 A4
Tilbrook Ind Est MK7 . . . . . . 37 C1
Tilbrook Rdbt MK7. . . . . 47 C4
Tilers Rd MK11 . . . . 24 B4
Tiller Ct LU7. . . . . 67 A1
Tillman Ct MK12 . . . . 18 A3
Timber La MK17 . . . . 51 A1
Timberscombe MK4 . . . . 34 B1
Timbold Dr MK7. . . . . 30 A1
Timor Ct MK11 . . . . 16 B4
Tindall Ave LU7. . . . . 66 B3
Tingewick Rd MK18. . . . . 74 A4
Tingewick Road Ind Est
  MK18. . . . . 74 A4
Tintagel Ct MK6 . . . . 28 A4
Tippet Cl MK7. . . . . 38 B2
Titchmarsh Ct MK6 . . . . 27 B2
Tiverton Cres MK4. . . . . 42 C3
Tolcarne Ave MK6 . . . . 28 A3
Tompkins Cl MK5. . . . . 33 C1
Tongwell La MK15,MK16. . . 12 B4
Tongwell Rdbt MK15 . . . . . . 12 C2
Tongwell St
  Milton Keynes,Broughton
    MK10. . . . . 23 B1
  Milton Keynes,Northfield
    MK15. . . . . 23 A3
  Milton Keynes,Pineham MK15. . 13 A1
  Walnut Tree MK7 . . . . 38 A4
Toot Hill Cl MK5 . . . . 33 B3
Top Angel MK18 . . . . 74 C1
Top Mdw MK7 . . . . 37 C1
Torre Cl MK3 . . . . 45 B4
Torridon Ct MK2. . . . . 55 A2
Towan Ave Fishermead MK6 . . 28 A2
  Milton Keynes MK6. . . . . 28 A3

Towcester Rd
Buckingham MK18 . . . . **71** A4
Old Stratford MK19 . . . . **6** A1
Tower Cres MK14 . . . . **21** A4
Tower Dr MK14 . . . . **54** C1
Townsend Gr MK13 . . . . **10** A2
Trafalgar Ave MK3 . . . . **44** C4
Tranlands Brigg MK13 . . . . . **19** C2
Travell Ct MK13 . . . . **19** C1
Travis Gr MK3 . . . . **45** B2
Treborough MK4 . . . . **44** B4
Tredington Gr MK7 . . . . **37** C2
Treefields MK18 . . . . **75** A4
Tremayne Ct MK6 . . . . **28** A2
Trent Dr MK16 . . . . **3** C2
Trentishoe Cres MK4 . . . . . . **34** B1
Trent Rd MK3 . . . . **44** C3
Trent Way LU7 . . . . **71** A3
Tresham Ct MK5 . . . . **26** A1
Trevithick La MK5 . . . . **33** C3
Trevone Ct MK6 . . . . **28** A2
Trinity Cl MK19 . . . . **6** A1
Trinity Rd MK12 . . . . **8** A1
Trispen Ct MK6 . . . . **28** A2
Troutbeck MK6 . . . . **28** C2
Trubys Gdn MK6 . . . . **28** A1
Trueman Pl MK6 . . . . **27** C2
Trumpton La MK7 . . . . **30** C1
Trunk Furlong MK17 . . . . **40** B4
Tudeley Hale MK7 . . . . **30** B2
Tudor Ct 5 LU7 . . . . **65** C1
Tudor Gdns MK11 . . . . **16** C2
Tuffnell Ct MK15 . . . . **13** A1
Tulla Ct MK2 . . . . **54** C2
Tummell Way MK2 . . . . **54** C4
Tunbridge Gr MK7 . . . . **30** B2
Turnberry Cl MK3 . . . . **44** B1
Turners Mews MK14 . . . . **21** A4
Turneys Dr MK12 . . . . **17** B4
Turnmill Ave MK6 . . . . **28** B4
Turnmill Ct MK6 . . . . **28** B4
Turnpike Ct MK17 . . . . **39** B3
Turnpike Rd MK43 . . . . **41** C1
Turpyn Ct MK6 . . . . **29** A2
Turvill End MK5 . . . . **26** B2
Tweed Dr MK3 . . . . **44** B3
Twinflower MK7 . . . . **37** C4
Twitchen La MK4 . . . . **34** B1
Two Mile Ash Mid Sch
MK8 . . . . **25** B3
Twyford La MK7 . . . . **38** A3
Tyburn Ave MK6 . . . . **28** B4
Tylers Gn MK3 . . . . **20** B1
Tynemouth Rise 3 MK10 . . **30** A3
Tyne Sq MK3 . . . . **44** B3
Tyrell Ct MK18 . . . . **74** B3
Tyrells Gdns MK17 . . . . **58** A2
Tyrells Rd MK17 . . . . **58** A2
Tyrill MK14 . . . . **10** B1
Tyson Pl MK6 . . . . **27** B2

U

Ullswater Dr LU7 . . . . **64** C1
Ulverscroft MK10 . . . . **30** B4
Ulyett Pl MK6 . . . . **27** B2
Underwood Pl MK6 . . . . **27** B2
Union St MK16 . . . . **3** C3
Univ of Buckingham
Buckingham MK18 . . . . **74** B3
Buckingham MK18 . . . . **74** B4
Univ of Buckingham (Verney
Pk) MK18 . . . . **75** A3
Upper Coombe LU7 . . . . **65** B2
Upper Fifth St MK9 . . . . **27** A4
Upper Fourth St MK9 . . . . . . **27** A4
Upper Second St MK9 . . . . . **27** A3
Upper Stonehayes MK14 . . . **11** B2
Upper Third St MK9 . . . . **27** A3
Upper Way MK17 . . . . **59** B4
Upper Weald MK19 . . . . **24** A2

Upper Wood Cl
1 Shenley Brook End MK5 . . . . **33** B1
Milton Keynes MK5 . . . . **33** A1
Upton Gr MK5 . . . . **34** A2

V

Vache La MK5 . . . . **33** A4
Valens Cl MK8 . . . . **25** B1
Valentine Ct MK8 . . . . **25** B1
Valerian Pl MK16 . . . . **2** B2
Valley Rd MK18 . . . . **75** B4
Van Der Bilt Ct MK13 . . . . **19** A4
Vandyke Cl MK17 . . . . **39** C4
Vandyke Rd LU7 . . . . **66** C4
Vandyke Upper Sch & Com
Coll LU7 . . . . **66** C3
Vantage Ct MK16 . . . . **4** B1
Vauxhall MK13 . . . . **19** C4
Vellan Ave MK6 . . . . **28** B3
Venables La MK15 . . . . **12** A1
Venetian Ct MK7 . . . . **30** C1
Verdi Cl MK7 . . . . **38** B3
Verdon Dr MK15 . . . . **12** A1
Verity Pl MK6 . . . . **27** C3
Verley Cl MK6 . . . . **28** C2
Vermont Pl MK15 . . . . **12** B3
Verney Cl MK18 . . . . **72** C1
Vernier Cres MK5 . . . . **32** C3
Veryan Pl MK6 . . . . **28** B3
Vicarage Gdns
Leighton Buzzard LU7 . . . . **69** B4
Milton Keynes MK13 . . . . **19** B2
Vicarage Rd
Leighton Buzzard LU7 . . . . **69** B4
Milton Keynes,Bradwell
MK13 . . . . **19** B2
Milton Keynes,Fenny Stratford
MK2 . . . . **46** C2
Milton Keynes,Stony Stratford
MK13 . . . . **16** B4
Vicarage St MK17 . . . . **40** A2
Vicarage Wlk MK11 . . . . **16** B4
Victoria Rd
Leighton Buzzard LU7 . . . . **69** B4
Milton Keynes MK2 . . . . **46** C3
Victoria Row MK18 . . . . **74** C4
Victoria St MK12 . . . . **18** B4
Victoria Terr MK17 . . . . **67** A1
Victory Ct MK1 . . . . **45** C4
Vienna Gr MK13 . . . . **18** C4
Village Ct LU7 . . . . **69** A4
Villiers Ct MK18 . . . . **71** A2
Vimy Ct LU7 . . . . **65** C1
Vimy Rd LU7 . . . . **65** C1
Vincent Ave MK8 . . . . **25** C2
Vintners Mews MK14 . . . . **21** A4
Virginia MK6 . . . . **28** A1
Viscount Way MK2 . . . . **46** A3
Volta Rise MK5 . . . . **34** A2
Vyne Cres MK5 . . . . **25** C3

W

Waddesdon Cl 8 MK8 . . . . . . **25** C2
Wadesmill La MK7 . . . . **37** B2
Wadhurst La MK10 . . . . **30** B3
Wadworth Holme MK10 . . . . . **22** C1
Wagner Cl MK7 . . . . **38** A2
Waine Ct MK18 . . . . **74** C3
Wainers Croft MK12 . . . . **17** C2
Wakefield Cl MK14 . . . . **11** B1
Walbank Gr MK5 . . . . **33** B1
Walbrook Ave MK6 . . . . **21** C1
Walgrave Dr MK13 . . . . **19** C2
Walker Ave MK12 . . . . **17** B4
Walkhampton Ave MK13 . . . . **20** A1
Wallace St MK13 . . . . **9** A1
Wallinger Dr MK5 . . . . **33** B1
Wallingford MK13 . . . . **19** C3
Wallmead Gdns MK5 . . . . **26** B1
Walney Pl MK4 . . . . **43** A3
Walnut Ct MK16 . . . . **2** C1
Walnut Dr
Maids Moreton MK18 . . . . **71** B4

Walnut Dr continued
Milton Keynes MK2 . . . . **46** C2
Walnuts Sch The MK6 . . . . . . **36** C3
Walnuts The LU7 . . . . **66** B4
Walnut Tree Rdbt MK7 . . . . . **30** C1
Walsh's Manor MK14 . . . . **10** C1
Waltham Dr MK10 . . . . **30** A3
Waltham Ho 4 MK3 . . . . **45** A3
Walton Dr MK7 . . . . **37** A4
Walton End MK7 . . . . **38** A4
Walton Heath MK3 . . . . **44** B1
Walton High Sch MK7 . . . . . . **38** A4
Walton Park Rdbt MK7 . . . . . **37** C2
Walton Rd Caldecotte MK7 . . . **37** C1
Milton Keynes MK10 . . . . **30** A4
Walton MK7 . . . . **37** C4
Wavendon MK10,MK17 . . . . **31** A1
Wandlebury MK14 . . . . **11** C2
Wandsworth Pl MK13 . . . . **20** B1
Wardle Pl MK6 . . . . **27** B2
Ward Rd MK1 . . . . **36** C1
Wardstone End MK4 . . . . **43** C4
Warmington Gdns MK15 . . . . **21** C3
Warneford Way LU7 . . . . **70** C3
Warners Cl MK17 . . . . **59** C3
Warners Rd MK17 . . . . **53** A1
Warren Bank MK6 . . . . **36** C3
Warren Cl MK18 . . . . **75** A3
Warren Yd MK12 . . . . **17** B4
Warwick Pl MK3 . . . . **44** C1
Warwick Rd MK3 . . . . **45** A1
Washfield MK4 . . . . **34** B1
Wastel MK6 . . . . **35** C3
Watchcroft Dr MK18 . . . . **71** A2
Watchet Ct MK4 . . . . **34** B1
Waterborne Wlk
7 Leighton Buzzard LU7 . . . . . **66** A1
Leighton Buzzard LU7 . . . . **65** C1
Water Cl MK19 . . . . **6** A1
Waterdell LU7 . . . . **66** C1
Water Eaton Rd MK2,MK3 . . . **46** A1
Waterford Cl MK3 . . . . **44** C3
Waterhall Comb Sch MK2 . . . **55** A2
Waterhouse Cl MK16 . . . . **3** C2
Water La LU7 . . . . **65** C1
Waterloo Ct MK3 . . . . **44** C4
Waterloo Rd LU7 . . . . **69** B4
Waterlow Ct MK16 . . . . **12** B4
Waterside MK6 . . . . **28** C2
Waterside Pk MK12 . . . . **8** B1
Watermeet Cl MK4 . . . . **34** B2
Watling St Bletchley MK2 . . . . **46** B3
Bow Brickhill MK17 . . . . **47** A2
Granby MK5 . . . . **35** B1
Milton Keynes,Kiln Farm MK8,
MK11 . . . . **24** B4
Milton Keynes,Shenley Lodge
MK6 . . . . **34** A4
Watling Terr MK2 . . . . **46** C3
Watlow Gdns MK18 . . . . **71** A2
Watson Cl MK8 . . . . **32** B4
Watten MK2 . . . . **55** B2
Wavell Ct MK15 . . . . **12** A1
Wavendon CE Fst Sch
MK17 . . . . **31** B1
Wavendon Fields MK17 . . . . . **39** A4
Wavendon Gate Comb Sch
MK7 . . . . **38** B4
Waveney Ct MK16 . . . . **4** A1
Waverley Croft MK10 . . . . **30** A3
Wealdstone Pl MK6 . . . . **28** A4
Weasel La MK3 . . . . **52** C4
Weathercock Cl MK17 . . . . . . **39** C3
Weathercock La MK17 . . . . . . **40** A2
Weavers Hill MK11 . . . . **17** B2
Webber Heath MK7 . . . . **38** B2
Webbs Home Cl MK10 . . . . . . **30** A4
Websters Mdw MK4 . . . . **44** A3
Wedgwood Ave MK14 . . . . . . **11** C3
Welbeck Cl MK10 . . . . **29** C3
Welburn Gr MK4 . . . . **43** C4
Weldon Rise MK5 . . . . **26** B2
Welland Dr MK16 . . . . **4** A1
Welland Ho MK3 . . . . **44** C2
Wellfield Ct MK15 . . . . **12** C2

Wellhayes MK14 . . . . **11** B2
Wellington Ho LU7 . . . . **62** C2
Wellington Pl MK3 . . . . **45** C1
Wells Ct 1 LU7 . . . . **66** A1
Wellsmead Fst Sch MK3 . . . . **45** A3
Wellsmead Mid Sch MK3 . . . **44** C4
Well St MK18 . . . . **74** C4
Welsummer Gr MK5 . . . . **33** B1
Wenning La MK4 . . . . **43** C4
Wentworth Dr LU7 . . . . **66** A2
Wentworth Way MK3 . . . . **44** A1
Werth Dr MK17 . . . . **49** C4
Westborne St MK13 . . . . **19** B4
Westbrook End MK17 . . . . **52** C1
Westbury Cl MK16 . . . . **3** A2
Westbury La MK16 . . . . **2** C3
Westcliffe MK8 . . . . **24** C4
Westcroft Rdbt MK4 . . . . **43** B4
West Dales MK13 . . . . **20** A3
Western Ave MK18 . . . . **72** B1
Western Rd
Milton Keynes,Fenny Stratford
MK2 . . . . **46** B3
Milton Keynes,Wolverton
MK12 . . . . **18** A4
Westfield Ave MK19 . . . . **14** B3
Westfield Rd MK2 . . . . **46** A1
Westfields MK18 . . . . **74** B4
West Hill MK17 . . . . **40** B2
Westhill MK14 . . . . **10** C2
Westminster Dr MK3 . . . . **45** B4
Westmorland Ho MK3 . . . . . . **45** A4
Weston Ave LU7 . . . . **70** C4
West Rd MK17 . . . . **39** C3
Westside LU7 . . . . **66** A1
West St Buckingham MK18 . . . **72** B1
Leighton Buzzard LU7 . . . . **65** C1
West Wlk MK9 . . . . **27** B4
Westwood Cl MK8 . . . . **25** C2
Wetherby Gdns MK3 . . . . **53** A4
Whaddon Rd
Milton Keynes,Shenley Brook
End MK5 . . . . **33** B1
Milton Keynes,Westcroft
MK4 . . . . **43** A4
Newport Pagnell MK16 . . . . **3** A1
Newton Longville MK17 . . . . . . **53** A1
Whaddon Way MK13 . . . . **45** A4
Whalley Dr MK3 . . . . **45** B4
Wharf Cl MK19 . . . . **6** A1
Wharf La MK19 . . . . **6** B1
Wharfside MK2 . . . . **46** C3
Wharfside Pl MK18 . . . . **71** A1
Wharf The
Milton Keynes,Giffard Park
MK14 . . . . **11** A4
Milton Keynes MK2 . . . . **55** B4
Wharf View MK18 . . . . **71** A1
Wheatcroft Cl MK6 . . . . **35** B3
Wheatfield Cl LU7 . . . . **67** A1
Wheatley Cl MK4 . . . . **44** A4
Wheelers La MK13 . . . . **19** B4
Wheelwright Mews MK14 . . . **21** A4
Wheelwrights Way MK19 . . . . . **6** B1
Whet Stone Cl MK13 . . . . **19** C2
Whichford MK14 . . . . **11** C3
Whitby Cl MK3 . . . . **45** B4
White Alder MK12 . . . . **18** C3
Whitebaker Ct MK14 . . . . **21** A4
Whitegate Ct MK6 . . . . **35** C4
Whitehall Ave MK10 . . . . **31** A3
White Horse Ct LU7 . . . . **66** A1
White Horse Dr MK4 . . . . **44** A4
Whitehorse Yd MK11 . . . . **16** B3
Whiteley Cres MK3 . . . . **53** C4
White Spire Sch MK3 . . . . **45** A3
Whitethorns MK16 . . . . **3** A1
Whitney Rdbt MK4 . . . . **42** C4
Whitsun Pasture MK15 . . . . . **12** A1
Whittington Chase MK4 . . . . . **42** C3
Whitton Way MK16 . . . . **3** B1
Whitworth La MK5 . . . . **26** B1
Wickstead Ave MK8 . . . . **32** B4
Wildacre Rd MK5 . . . . **33** B2
Wilford Cl MK15 . . . . **28** C4

Wilks Croft MK5 . . . . .25 C1
Willen Comb Sch MK15 . . . . . .12 B1
Willen La MK14 . . . . .11 B2
Willen Park Ave MK15 . . . . . .21 C4
Willen Rd
  Milton Keynes MK10 . . . . .23 A1
  Newport Pagnell MK16 . . . . .3 C1
Willets Rise MK5 . . . . .33 B3
Willey Cl MK11 . . . . .17 A2
Williams Circ MK7 . . . . .37 B2
William Smith Cl MK15 . . . . . .22 A1
William Sutton Ho MK5 . . . . .33 B4
Willow Bank Wlk LU7 . . . . . .66 C2
Willow Dr MK18 . . . . .75 B3
Willowford MK13 . . . . .18 C3
Willow Gr MK19 . . . . .15 C4
Willow Ho LU7 . . . . .65 B1
Willow La MK11 . . . . .16 A3
Willows First Sch The MK6 . .28 A4
Willows The LU7 . . . . .70 B4
Willow Way MK2 . . . . .46 A1
Willow Wren MK14 . . . . .11 B4
Wilmin Gr MK5 . . . . .26 B1
Wilsley Pound MK7 . . . . .30 B2
Wilson Cl MK8 . . . . .25 B1
Wilton Ave MK3 . . . . .45 B2
Wiltshire Way MK3 . . . . .44 C3
Wimbledon Pl MK13 . . . . .20 B1
Wimblington Dr MK6 . . . . . . .35 B2
Wimborne Cres MK4 . . . . . . .43 A4
Wincanton Hill MK3 . . . . .52 C4
Winchester Circ MK10 . . . . . .30 B3
Windermere Dr MK2 . . . . .55 A3
Windermere Gdns LU7 . . . . .64 C1
Windmill Cl MK18 . . . . .71 B1
Windmill Hill Dr MK3 . . . . . . .44 A3
Windmill Hill Rdbt MK4 . . . . .44 A3
Windmill Path ⑤ LU7 . . . . . .66 A1
Windrush Cl MK15 . . . . .21 B4

Windsor Ave
  Leighton Buzzard LU7 . . . . .65 C1
  Newport Pagnell MK16 . . . . .3 B2
Windsor St
  Milton Keynes MK2 . . . . .46 A1
  Milton Keynes,Wolverton
    MK12 . . . . .18 A4
Winfold La MK4 . . . . .43 C3
Wingate Circ MK7 . . . . .37 B2
Wingfield Gr MK10 . . . . .30 A4
Wing Rd LU7 . . . . .69 A3
Winsford Hill MK4 . . . . .34 C1
Winstanley La MK5 . . . . .34 A2
Winston Cl LU7 . . . . .66 A3
Winterburn MK13 . . . . .19 C3
Winwood Cl MK19 . . . . .14 C3
Wisewood Rd MK4,MK5 . . . . .32 C2
Wishart Gn MK7 . . . . .38 C3
Wisley Ave MK13 . . . . .20 B1
Wistmans MK4 . . . . .34 B2
Witan Ct MK9 . . . . .27 A4
Witan Gate MK9 . . . . .27 A3
Witham St MK3 . . . . .44 B3
Withington MK13 . . . . .19 B3
Withycombe MK4 . . . . .34 C1
Wittmills Oak MK18 . . . . .71 A1
Woad La MK14 . . . . .11 A2
Woburn Ave MK12 . . . . .18 A4
Woburn Ct LU7 . . . . .69 B4
Woburn La MK17 . . . . .40 C2
Woburn Lower Sch MK17 . . . .51 A1
Woburn Pl LU7 . . . . .66 A3
Woburn Rd
  Aspley Heath MK17 . . . . .50 A4
  Little Brickhill MK17 . . . . .57 B4
Woburn Sands Rd MK17 . . . . .38 B1
Woburn Sands Sta MK17 . . . . .39 B3
Wodehouse Wlk MK16 . . . . . . .2 C3
Wolfscote La MK4 . . . . .33 C1

Wolsey Gdns MK13 . . . . .19 B2
Wolston Mdw MK10 . . . . .23 A1
Wolverton Rd
  Milton Keynes,Gifford Park
    MK16 . . . . .11 A4
  Milton Keynes,Stony Stratford
    MK11 . . . . .16 C4
  Milton Keynes,Wolverton MK12,
    MK19 . . . . .9 A2
  Newport Pagnell MK16 . . . . .3 A2
Wolverton Sta MK19 . . . . .9 A1
Woodall Cl MK10 . . . . .22 C1
Wood End Fst Sch MK14 . . . .10 C2
Woodhouse Ct MK14 . . . . .20 B4
Wood La Aspley Guise MK17 . . .40 B2
  Milton Keynes MK14 . . . . .11 A2
Woodland Ave LU7 . . . . .65 C4
Woodland Cl LU7 . . . . .62 C3
Woodlands Cl MK18 . . . . .71 A2
Woodlands Cres MK18 . . . . . .72 C2
Woodland View MK12 . . . . . . .18 B3
Woodland Way MK17 . . . . . . .39 C2
Woodley Headland MK6 . . . . .28 C1
Woodman Cl LU7 . . . . .66 B1
Woodmans Cl MK19 . . . . .14 C2
Woodruff Ave MK14 . . . . .20 C2
Woodrush Cl MK6 . . . . .35 C2
Woodside
  Aspley Guise MK17 . . . . .40 B1
  Milton Keynes MK11 . . . . .16 C4
Woodside Way LU7 . . . . .69 A4
Woodspring Cl MK10 . . . . . . .29 C3
Wood St MK13 . . . . .9 B1
Woodstock Ct MK13 . . . . .10 A1
Wood St MK17 . . . . .39 C2
Wood The LU7 . . . . .66 A2
Woodward Ho ④ MK2 . . . . . .46 A2
Woodward Pl MK8 . . . . .26 A3

Woolmans
  Fullers Slade MK11 . . . . .17 B2
  Milton Keynes MK11 . . . . .17 B2
Woolrich Gdns MK11 . . . . .16 C3
Worcester Cl MK16 . . . . .2 C1
Worcester Ho MK3 . . . . .45 A4
Wordsworth Ave MK16 . . . . . .2 C2
Wordsworth Dr MK3 . . . . .45 B1
Worrelle Ave MK10 . . . . .23 B1
Wray Ct MK4 . . . . .43 B4
Wren Cl MK18 . . . . .75 B3
Wrens Pk MK10 . . . . .30 B4
Wroxton Ct MK4 . . . . .43 A4
Wye Cl MK3 . . . . .44 C3
Wylie End MK13 . . . . .9 C1
Wymondham MK10 . . . . .30 B3
Wyness Ave MK17 . . . . .57 B3
Wyngates LU7 . . . . .69 B3
Wynyard Ct MK6 . . . . .27 B1
Wyvern Fst Sch MK12 . . . . . .18 A4

Y

Yalts Brow MK4 . . . . .43 C4
Yardley Rd MK19 . . . . .6 C3
Yarrow Pl MK14 . . . . .20 C2
Yeats Cl MK16 . . . . .2 B3
Yeomans Dr MK14 . . . . .12 A3
Yew Tree Cl MK17 . . . . .52 C1
Yew Tree Ct ⑧ LU7 . . . . .66 A1
Yonder Slade MK18 . . . . .74 C2
York Ct ⑧ LU7 . . . . .65 C1
York Ho MK3 . . . . .44 C1
York Rd MK11 . . . . .16 B3
Young Ind Est LU7 . . . . .71 A4

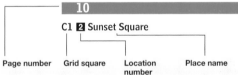

List of numbered locations

In some busy areas of the maps it is not always possible to show the name of every place.

Where not all names will fit, some smaller places are shown by a number. If you wish to find out the name associated with a number, use this listing.

The places in this list are also listed normally in the Index.

10

C1 **2** Sunset Square

Page number   Grid square   Location number   Place name

25

C2 **2** Mentmore Ct
   3 Sulgrave Ct
   4 Houghton Ct
   5 Rushton Ct
   6 Huntingbrooke
   8 Waddeson Cl
C3 **1** Portchester Ct
   2 Petworth Ho
   3 Albury Ct
   4 Corsham Ct
   5 Bowood Ct
   7 Longleat Ct
   8 Peckover Ct
   9 Hogarths Ct

27

B3 **1** Appleyard Pl
   2 Richardson Pl
   3 Leyland Pl
   4 Barrington Mews

30

A3 **1** Pershore Croft
   2 Stavordale
   3 Tynemouth Rise
   4 Leominster Gate

B3 **1** Launde
   2 St Botolphs

33

B1 **1** Upper Wood Cl
C1 **1** Alstonefield
   2 Gillamoor Cl
   3 Fadmoor Pl
   4 Appleton Mews

43

C4 **1** Grosmont Cl
   2 Goathland Croft
   3 Little Habton
   4 Lowick Pl
   5 Stagshaw Gr
   6 Tarnbrook Cl
   7 Hazelhurst

44

A4 **1** Greystonley
   2 Denchworth Ct
   3 Marshaw Pl
   4 Fernborough Haven
   5 Sparsholt Cl
B3 **1** Hungerford Ho
   2 Ashburnham Cl
   3 Hollinwell Cl

45

A3 **1** Durham Ho
   2 Pembroke Ho
   3 Rutland Ho
   4 Waltham Ho
   5 Sawley Ho
   6 Norfolk Ho
   7 Flint Ho

46

A2 **1** Alexander Ho
   2 Lee Ho
   3 Christine Ho
   4 Woodward Ho
   5 Stanier Sq
   6 Concourse The
   7 Agora Ctr

65

B1 **1** Springfield Ct
   2 Springside
   3 Rockleigh Ct
   4 Park View Ct
   5 Castle Ho
   6 Chelsea Ho
C1 **1** Basildon Ct
   2 Kilgour Ct
   3 York Ct

   4 Rosebery Ct
   5 Tudor Ct
   6 Ropa Ct
C2 **1** Ashwell St
   2 Mill Rd
   3 Croxley Ct

66

A1 **1** Wells Ct
   2 Old School Ct
   3 Yew Tree Ct
   4 Hamilton Ct
   5 Windmill Path
   6 Peacock Mews
   7 Waterborne Wlk
   8 Market Mews
   9 Bell Alley
   10 Leck Ho
A2 **1** Lamsey Ct
   2 Chapel Path
   3 Barrow Path
   4 Ashwell Place
   5 Page's Almshouses
   6 Gilbert Mews
   7 Adaern Cl

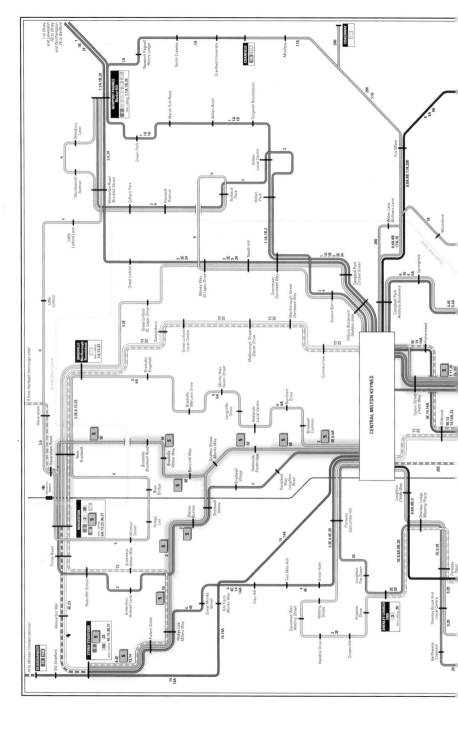

II

Key to map symbols

Roads

(12)	**Motorway** with junction number
A42	**Primary route** – dual/single carriageway
A42	**A road** – dual/single carriageway
B1289	**B road** – dual/single carriageway
	Through-route – dual/single carriageway
	Minor road – dual/single carriageway
	Rural track, private road or narrow road in urban area
	Path, bridleway, byway open to all traffic, road used as a public path
	Road under construction
	Pedestrianised area
	Gate or obstruction to traffic restrictions may not apply at all times or to all vehicles
P P&R	**Parking, Park and Ride**

Railways

	Railway
	Miniature railway
	Metro station, private railway station

Emergency services

	Ambulance station, coastguard station
	Fire station, police station
H +	**Hospital, Accident and Emergency entrance to hospital**

General features

+ PO	**Place of worship, Post Office**
i	**Information centre** (open all year)
	Bus, coach station
	Important buildings, schools, colleges, universities and hospitals
	Woods, built-up area
Tumulus FORT	**Non-Roman antiquity, Roman antiquity**

Leisure facilities

	Camping site, caravan site
	Golf course, picnic site

Boundaries

• • • • • • • •	**Postcode boundaries**
	County and unitary authority boundaries

Water features

River Ouse	**Tidal water, water name**
	Non-tidal water – lake, river, canal or stream
< I	**Lock, weir**

Scales

4½ inches to 1 mile 1:14 080

0	220 yds	¼ mile	660 yds	½ mile

0	125m	250m	375m	½ km

74	**Adjoining page indicators** The mapping continues on the page indicated by the arrow

Abbreviations

Acad	Academy	Mkt	Market
Allot Gdns	Allotments	Meml	Memorial
Cemy	Cemetery	Mon	Monument
C Ctr	Civic Centre	Mus	Museum
CH	Club House	Obsy	Observatory
Coll	College	Pal	Royal Palace
Crem	Crematorium	PH	Public House
Ent	Enterprise	Recn Gd	Recreation Ground
Ex H	Exhibition Hall	Resr	Reservoir
Ind Est	Industrial Estate	Ret Pk	Retail Park
IRB Sta	Inshore Rescue Boat Station	Sch	School
		Sh Ctr	Shopping Centre
Inst	Institute	TH	Town Hall/House
Ct	Law Court	Trad Est	Trading Estate
L Ctr	Leisure Centre	Univ	University
LC	Level Crossing	Wks	Works
Liby	Library	YH	Youth Hostel

STREET ATLAS
Milton Keynes
and Buckingham

First published 2006 by

Philip's, a division of
Octopus Publishing Group Ltd
2–4 Heron Quays
London E14 4JP

First edition 2006
First impression 2006

ISBN-10   0-540-08919-2
ISBN-13   978-0-540-08919-2
© Philip's 2006

o|s Ordnance Survey®

This product includes mapping data licensed
from Ordnance Survey®, with the
permission of the Controller of Her Majesty's
Stationery Office.© Crown copyright 2006.
All rights reserved.
Licence number 100011710

To the best of the Publishers' knowledge, the
information in this atlas was correct at the
time of going to press. No responsibility can
be accepted for any errors or their
consequences.

The representation in this atlas of a road,
track or path is no evidence of the existence
of a right of way.

Ordnance Survey and the OS symbol are
registered trademarks of Ordnance Survey,
the national mapping agency of Great Britain

Photographic acknowledgements:
IX Robert Stainforth / Alamy
X Nick Hawkes / Alamy

Printed by Toppan, China

Contents

II **Key to map symbols**

III **Key to map pages**

IV **Route planning**

VIII **Sights of Milton Keynes**

2 **Street maps** at 4½ inches to 1 mile

76 **Index**

91 **List of numbered locations**

92 **Milton Keynes bus map**